WAR DIARY OF THE FIFTH SEAFORTH HIGH-LANDERS 51st (HIGHLAND) DIVISION

WITH ILLUSTRATIONS AND A MAP
BY CAPTAIN D. SUTHERLAND, M.C., T.D.

LONDON: JOHN LANE, THE BODLEY HEAD, W.
NEW YORK: JOHN LANE COMPANY MCMXX

PRINTED BY MORRISON AND GIBB LIMITED, EDINBURGH

TO

THE OFFICERS

NON-COMMISSIONED OFFICERS AND MEN

OF THE FIFTH SEAFORTH HIGHLANDERS

CONTENTS

WAR DIARY OF THE FIFTH SEAFORTH HIGHLANDERS

CHAPTER I

INTRODUCTORY

THE 5th Seaforth Highlanders, whose war record is given in this book, is the Territorial Battalion of Caithness and Sutherland, the two most northerly counties in Scotland.

The battalion was first formed in 1859, early in the Volunteer movement, by the Duke of Sutherland and took as its badge, the Sutherland Crest (the Wild Cat), with the proud motto " Sans Peur," while its tartan was also the Sutherland, of black, navy blue, and green, similar to that worn by the Argyll and Sutherland Highlanders.

At first confined to Sutherlandshire, it later amalgamated with the Caithness Volunteers and was known as the 1st Sutherland Highland Rifle Volunteers.

It had a double justification for its badge and tartan, for the 93rd (Sutherland) Highlanders were recruited

A

in 1801, during the Napoleonic Wars, in the same area, and had the same badge and tartan, hence the battalion regards itself as the lineal descendant of that famous unit.

When the Territorial Force was formed, the battalion had to change its name to the 5th (Sutherland and Caithness) Seaforth Highlanders, but, as a concession to volunteer and county traditions, it was still allowed to wear the Sutherland Badge and Tartan, and is thus unique in being differently dressed from all other Seaforth Battalions.

On 5th August 1914 its mobilization, under Col. E. G. Buik, V.D., took place, the various companies concentrating at Nigg on the northern shore of the Cromarty Firth, whence, after a week spent in digging trenches for the defence of the Admiralty Forts on the North Sutor, it proceeded to Inverness.

Thence, in a few days, it entrained for Bedford, which became the training centre for the Highland Territorial Division, afterwards so well known as the 51st.

For eight months the Division was billeted in this town, and was treated with the utmost cordiality and kindness by the townspeople, who did all they could to make their kilted invaders comfortable and happy.

During these months several battalions were drafted to France at various times, but, owing to fears of invasion on the East Coast, the majority of the battalion were retained for home defence until April

INTRODUCTORY

1915, much to the disgust of officers and men who were chafing at their long delayed departure for the theatre of war.

At length in April 1915 came the news that the Division was to proceed overseas, new transport and equipment were provided, but unfortunately not new guns (Territorial Artillery units were still considered sufficiently well armed with the old converted 13-pounders), and on 1st May the battalion entrained for Folkestone.

During this period the battalion had been broken up into 1st and 2nd line units, the latter consisting of those unfit for overseas work, or who had not yet realized the necessity of volunteering for foreign service, and the numbers required for the overseas battalion had been obtained by voluntary recruiting, not only in Scotland but also in London and other parts of England.

The battalion was in France from 1st May 1915 until its cadre returned to headquarters at Golspie in April 1919, during which time it bore its own share in all the fierce engagements taken part in by the 51st Division.

As a proof of its arduous work during that time there passed through the battalion 221 officers and 5331 N.C.O.'s and men, while its casualties were :—

	Killed.	Wounded.	Missing.	
Officers	29	94	9	(All presumed killed).
Other Ranks	701	2391	291	(Majority presumed killed).

Its share of honours was also considerable, being as follows :—

1/5th Battalion Seaforth Highlanders

DECORATIONS[1]

———◆———

OFFICERS

DISTINGUISHED SERVICE ORDER

	AUTHORITY. London Gazette.
*Major J. J. ROBERTSON . . .	10/1/1917
A/Lieut.-Col. W. MORRISON, M.C., D.C.M. (Gordon Highlanders att.) . .	15/10/1918

MILITARY CROSS

*Capt. D. SUTHERLAND (att. R.E. Signals) .	14/1/1916
Lieut. E. A. MACKINTOSH . . .	27/5/1916
2nd Lieut. F. LUPTON . . .	10/1/1917
*2nd Lieut. A. J. MACKAY . . .	,, ,,
*2nd Lieut. A. J. MACKAY (Bar) . .	26/7/1917
*2nd Lieut. T. F. GRANT . . .	,, ,,
2nd Lieut. D. SIMPSON . . .	,, ,,
2nd Lieut. J. A. INNES . . .	26/9/1917
A/Capt. I. MACKENZIE . . .	4/2/1918
2nd Lieut. J. L. BYRNE . . .	,, ,,
2nd Lieut. D. D. CAIRNIE . . .	,, ,,
Lieut. J. R. BLACK	1/1/1918
*Lieut. T. F. GRANT (Bar) . . .	26/7/1918
Lieut. J. B. SIMPSON . . .	,, ,,
Lieut. D. STEWART	,, ,,
2nd Lieut. F. W. JAGGARD . . .	,, ,,

[1] * More than one Decoration.

4

INTRODUCTORY

AUTHORITY.
London Gazette.

	AUTHORITY. London Gazette.
Capt. G. A. SUTHERLAND . . .	11/5/1918
Capt. T. H. HAY-WILL (Bar. M.C. awarded with 4th Battalion; also Foreign Decoration) . . .	15/10/1918
*Lieut. W. W. NICOLSON . . .	,, ,,
2nd Lieut. G. M. D. CARSE . . .	,, ,,
2nd Lieut. J. MORRISON . . .	,, ,,
Lieut. W. THORBURN . . .	,, ,,
Lieut. F. H. M'GREGOR (U.S. M.C. att.) .	24/8/1918
*Capt. D. SUTHERLAND (att. R.E. Signals). (Bar)	26/7/1918
Lieut. G. H. DURES . . .	7/11/1918
2nd Lieut. T. S. HENNESSY . . .	8/3/1919
A/Capt. R. M. TAYLOR . . .	3/6/1919
A/Capt. W. BIRNIE . . .	,, ,,
Capt. the Rev. W. P. YOUNG, D.C.M. (A.C.D. att.)	,, ,,

MENTIONED IN DESPATCHES

Capt. and Adjt. N. C. ORR . . .	15/6/1916
Major J. J. ROBERTSON . . .	,, ,,
Major J. J. ROBERTSON . . .	25/5/1917
Capt. J. B. MORRISON . . .	,, ,,
Capt. the Rev. A. BOYD SCOTT (A.C.D. att.) .	29/5/1917
Lieut.-Col. J. M. SCOTT, D.S.O. (A. & S. H. att.)	21/12/1917
Capt. W. A. MACDONALD . . .	,, ,,
A/Capt. J. CORRIGALL . . .	,, ,,
A/Capt. C. A. MACKAY . . .	,, ,,
Lieut. W. A. BARNETSON . . .	24/5/1918
Lieut.-Col. W. MORRISON, D.S.O., M.C., D.C.M. (Gordon Highlanders att.) .	28/12/1918
A/Capt. W. BIRNIE . . .	,, ,,
Capt. D. SUTHERLAND . . .	1/1/1916

WAR DIARY OF THE FIFTH SEAFORTHS

FOREIGN DECORATIONS

AUTHORITY.
London Gazette.

*Lieut.-Col. J. M. SCOTT, D.S.O. (A. & S. H. att.). (Order of Leopold (Officier), Belgian) 26/9/1917

Major A. C. M'INTYRE, M.C. (A. & S.H. att.). (Belgian Croix de Guerre) . .   12/7/1918

*Lieut.-Col. J. M. SCOTT, D.S.O. (A. & S. H. att.). (Belgian Croix de Guerre) .   11/3/1918

*Lieut. W. W. NICOLSON (French Croix de Guerre) 8/9/1918

*Lieut.-Col. W. MORRISON, D.S.O., M.C., D.C.M. (Gordon Highlanders att.). (French Croix de Guerre) . .

Lieut.-Col. J. J. C. DAVIDSON, T.D. (Medaille Agricole (French)). . . .

OTHER RANKS

VICTORIA CROSS.

L/Cpl. R. M'BEATH 1/1/1918

MILITARY CROSS

C.S.M. W. MILLAR 19/8/1916

DISTINGUISHED CONDUCT MEDAL

R.S.M. D. SUTHERLAND. (See also Foreign Decoration) 14/1/1916

Dvr. R. BOCOCK . . . .   ,,   ,,

C.S.M. J. BRUCE . . . .   ,,   ,,

Sergt. J. DUCHART . . . .   ,,   ,,

C.S.M. R. MURRAY 3/6/1916

6

INTRODUCTORY

	AUTHORITY. London Gazette.
Sergt. A. MORRISON	26/7/1917
Sergt. J. MOWAT. (See also M.M.) . .	,, ,,
Sergt. A. MACKAY. (See also M.M.) .	22/10/1917
Sergt. T. MOORE	19/11/1917
Sergt. H. MATHESON. (See also M.M.) .	28/3/1918
Sergt. J. S. KELLY. (See also M.M.) .	1/1/1918
Sergt. G. DUNNETT. (See also M.S.M.) .	3/9/1918
Sergt. J. NEILSON . . .	,, ,,
L/Cpl. J. DUFFY. (See also M.M.) . .	,, ,,
Sergt. R. CROMARTY . .	,, ,,
Cpl. G. HOTCHKISS. (See also M.M.) .	,, ,,
Pte. W. ANDERSON. (See also M.M.) .	,, ,,
L/Cpl. J. SHAND	,, ,,
Sergt. J. MAYLON	3/6/1918
Sergt. S. V. WOOD	30/10/1918
Pte. J. KENNEDY	,, ,,
Pte. W. CROZIER	15/11/1918
Sergt. H. MACKENZIE (Bar. D.C.M. awarded with another Battalion) .	12/3/1919
Sergt. R. WEDDELL	1/1/1919
Sergt. R. F. JOHNSTONE . . .	3/6/1919

MILITARY MEDAL

L/Sergt. R. M. MORRISON . . .	27/5/1916
Pte. D. CAMERON	,, ,,
Pte. G. GRANT	,, ,,
Sergt. H. FRASER	3/6/1916
Sergt. R. W. GODDARD . . .	11/11/1916
Pte. G. FINDLAY	,, ,,
Sergt. R. W. GODDARD (Bar) . .	21/1/1917
Pte G. CORMACK	,, ,,
L/Sergt. D. COGHILL	,, ,,
L/Cpl. A. EWING	,, ,,
Sergt. W. A. GRANT	,, ,,
Pte. R. M'KENZIE	,, ,,

WAR DIARY OF THE FIFTH SEAFORTHS

	AUTHORITY. *London Gazette.*
Pte. J. G. M'Leod	21/1/1917
Cpl. R. More	,, ,,
L/Sergt. A. J. Paton	,, ,,
Pte. W. Roach	,, ,,
Pte. J. W. T. Strickland	,, ,,
Sergt. J. Elder	18/6/1917
Sergt. J. C. Stacey	,, ,,
Sergt. W. Murray	,, ,,
L/Sergt. J. Ross	,, ,,
Cpl. W. Mackay	,, ,,
L/Sergt. S. W. Lloyd	,, ,,
L/Sergt. R. Harper	,, ,,
L/Sergt. E. Bedford	,, ,,
L/Sergt. B. Rawlings	,, ,,
L/Sergt. W. Hamilton	,, ,,
L/Sergt. B. Donn	,, ,,
Sergt. A. Mackay (also D.C.M.)	9/7/1917
Pte. J. Johnson	,, ,,
Sergt. J. M'Leod	18/7/1917
L/Cpl. D. Rendall	,, ,,
L/Cpl. F. Cowie	,, ,,
Pte. J. Savage	,, ,,
Pte. W. A. Bull	,, ,,
Pte. S. Sinclair	,, ,,
Pte. A. Bremner	,, ,,
Pte. D. Sutherland	,, ,,
Pte. F. Lawrie	,, ,,
Pte. J. Pirrie	26/9/1917
Pte. W. Somerville	,, ,,
L/Cpl. W. M'Donald	,, ,,
L/Cpl W. Eyeval	,, ,,
Pte. S. O. Gibson	,, ,,
Cpl. J. Sutherland	,, ,,
Pte. W. E. M. Clarke	,, ,,
L/Cpl. J. Anderson	,, ,,
L/Cpl. W. Neat	,, ,,

INTRODUCTORY

9

	AUTHORITY. London Gazette.
Pte. J. SUTHERLAND .	2/8/1918
L/Cpl. D M. MACKAY	,, ,,
Sergt. G. GUNN	,, ,,
L/Sergt. W ARMSTRONG	,, ,,
L/Cpl. G. HOTCHKISS (also D.C.M.) .	,, ,,
Sergt. G. BARTLETT .	,, ,,
L/Cpl. A. CORMACK .	,, ,,
Pte. J. REID .	,, ,,
Pte. R. DEIGNAN	,, ,,
Pte. R. DEAN	,, ,,
Pte. W. MOORE	,, ,,
Pte. J. MACKAY	,, ,,
Pte. J. M'LAUGHLIN .	,, ,,
Pte. W. JACK	,, ,,
Pte. J. BOARDMAN	29/8/1918
Pte. W. BONNER	7/10/1918
L/Cpl. D. ELDER	,, ,,
Sgt. H. MATHESON (also D.C.M.)	,, ,,
L/Cpl. A. MUNRO	,, ,,
Pte. R. DURRAND	16/7/1918
Sergt. M. A. M'LEAN	,, ,,
Pte. R. DEAN (Bar) .	11/12/1918
Pte. J. G. M'LEOD (Bar)	,, ,,
Pte. F. FORREST	,, ,,
Pte. W. A. FALCONER	,, ,,
Pte. D. STEPHEN	,, ,,
Pte. A. PARR	,, ,,
L/Cpl. J. GORDON	,, ,,
Pte. J. CUTHBERTSON	,, ,,
L/Cpl. D. SUTHERLAND	,, ,,
Sergt. L. CROLL	,, ,,
Sergt. D. DAVIDSON .	,, ,,
Sergt. A. ATKIN	,, ,,
L/Cpl. D. MACKAY .	,, ,,
L/Cpl. G. HENDERSON	,, ,,
Pte. A. AIRD	,, ,,

INTRODUCTORY

MENTIONED IN DESPATCHES

11

WAR DIARY OF THE FIFTH SEAFORTHS

	AUTHORITY. *London Gazette.*
Pte. W. MACKAY	25/5/1917
C.Q.M.S. R. FORBES	21/12/1917
Sergt. R. F. JOHNSTONE . . .	,, ,,
Sergt. S. S. MILLER	,, ,,
Sergt. V. A. EARNSCLIFFE (att. 152 T.M.B.) .	,, ,,
L/Cpl. J. GUNN	24/5/1918
A/Cpl. F. NICHOLS	,, ,,
C.Q.M.S. R. FORBES	28/12/1918
Sergt. R. WEDDELL	,, ,,

MERITORIOUS SERVICE MEDALS

Suptg. Clerk J. GUNN . . .	4/6/1917
A/Sergt. H. STEEL	17/6/1918
Sergt. M. SHEARER	,, ,,
Sergt. G. DUNNETT (also D.C.M.) . .	,, ,,
Cpl. A. GREENWOOD	,, ,,
Sergt. A. DE' ATH	18/1/1919
A/L/Sergt. F. V. CHEESWRIGHT . .	,, ,,
A/Cpl. F. NICHOLS	,, ,,
A/L/Sergt. A. WHEELANS . . .	,, ,,

MEMBER OF BRITISH EMPIRE

Suptg. Clerk J. GUNN (also M.S.M.) .

FOREIGN DECORATIONS

R.S.M. D. SUTHERLAND (also D.C.M.) (French Croix de Guerre) . .	7/11/1915
C.S.M. J. FRASER (Belgian Croix de Guerre)	12/7/1918
Cpl. J. MACKAY (also M.M.) (French Croix de Guerre)	7/1/1919
L/Cpl. J. CALDWELL (French Croix de Guerre)	11/1/1919

INTRODUCTORY

AUTHORITY.
London Gazette.

Pte. M. MURPHY (also M.M.) (French Croix
de Guerre) 11/1/1919
Cpl. G. MURRAY (also M.M.) (French Croix
de Guerre) . . . . ,, ,,
Pte. J. HAY (Gordon Highlanders att.) (also
M.M.) (French Croix de Guerre) . ,, ,,
Pte. W. TAYLOR (French Croix de Guerre) . ,, ,,

CHAPTER II

MAY 1915—DECEMBER 1916

ON 1st May 1915 the battalion embarked at Folkestone and after an uneventful crossing landed at Boulogne.

After a night in a rest camp, more noted for cold than for comfort, entraining took place next day, and after a long, wearisome journey the battalion detrained at Merville, and marched to its billets at Robecq and the surrounding farms.

Lieut.-Col. J. J. C. Davidson, T.D., was in command of the battalion, with Major Don. Sinclair, V.D., as second in command, while Capt. N. C. Orr was Adjutant, the Company Commanders being Major A. L. Macmillan, T.D., and Capts. D. Manson, T.D., J. J. Robertson and D. W. Milligan, with Major Morrison, V.D., as Quartermaster, the battalion being at its full strength of 976 N.C.O.'s and men.

To the battalion this first train journey in France was very strange, the long slow crawl in the easy-going French train, the horse boxes in which the men travelled, the numerous stoppages at little village

14

stations, the cries of the French children for "Souvenir," " Biske," " Bouton," and then, as darkness fell, and the train approached nearer the front, the constant flashes of the guns, all combined to fix that first journey for ever in the mind of all.

The distant flashes brought to the mind of each that now we were coming to the reality for which we had been preparing so long, and that brought the thought, " Shall we be able to make good under the ordeal ? "—a thought which troubled us not a little.

Then the billeting in barns, stables, disused factories, and outhouses was also something new, while the French country people's ideas of sanitation and what constitutes a good source of drinking water were rather staggering to our hygienic principles, when one generally found the farm pump in close proximity to the farm manure heap.

At Robecq the battalion remained from the 4th to the 13th May, but on that day sudden orders came to move northward owing to the great German attempt to break through at Ypres, and on the morning of the 14th the whole Division was on the march and by evening the battalion was in billets at Strazeele, a little village between Hazebrouck and Bailleul. The situation in the north having improved, we remained here for four days.

This village had been in the hands of the Germans earlier in the war, and as the parish priest could not or would not hand over the keys of the church to them, they shot him and buried his body in a shallow grave in front of his church, and so carelessly was he buried that his legs were visible above the surface, until his parishioners gave him decent burial. On the night of the 18th we were again on the march, practically retracing our steps, and at dawn after a wearisome march along overcrowded muddy roads in a cold, driving rain we reached Vielle Chapelle, a small village close behind Neuve Chapelle where a fierce fight had been going on during the preceding few days, the British having attacked in order to relieve the pressure on Ypres. Here the battalion had its first experience under fire, for shortly after our arrival, the village was vigorously shelled, and Lieut. Miller and six men were badly wounded.

RICHEBOURG ST. VAAST

On the night of the 22nd the battalion took over the trenches from the 6th Seaforths and thus began its record of trench warfare which went on for several weary years.

Our sector was in front of Richebourg St. Vaast, formerly a nice little village on the Estaires—La Bassée Road, but now a mere collection of roofless ruins with shell-shattered walls crumbling up under the heavy German fire.

The conditions were not particularly enticing. Thousands of dead, both British and German, but mainly British, still lay on the ground covered by our advance of a few days before. The trenches were miserably constructed, compared to the elaborate trenches of later days. The shelters were of the most flimsy character, two or three beams, a bit of corrugated iron, and several inches of earth, while for some days battalion headquarters just behind the village had no other cover than a canvas sheet stretched across the trench.

When one thinks of it in the light of later experiences, one wonders how there were so comparatively few casualties, for the Germans pounded us with 5·9s, but "where ignorance is bliss, etc.," is a very useful proverb, and we took it all unconcernedly as part of the game.

Our first duty here was to convert the old German trench now in our hands, to dig a new front line trench several hundred yards further forward, and connect both and the village by new communication trenches, all which was satisfactorily carried out.

After coming out of the trenches on the 26th the battalion provided fatigue parties nightly until 31st May for trench improvement, and during that time buried 800 dead from the previous fight, a gruesome task which did not go down well with new troops.

FESTUBERT, JUNE 1916

On 31st May the Division sidestepped a few miles
further south, taking over the line in front and to the
north of Festubert. Here the area is very water-
logged, with deep ditches full of stagnant water and
built up parapets of earth faced and topped with
sandbags.

On 4th June the battalion occupied the reserve
trenches in front of Indian Village, so called from its
ruins having been held by Indian troops prior to our
coming. This was a much hotter corner even than
Richebourg, the Boche being much nearer, and having
better observation of the area behind our front line ;
with the result that any undue movement led to a
severe strafing.

A peculiarly odious salient was a part of our battalion
front called the Orchard which was continuously under
heavy cross fire, both machine and field gun, while to
get to it the men had to double across a ditch which
was in full view of the German machine gunners with
the result that there were always dead or wounded
lying there.

During this four days' spell, the battalion had one
officer, Captain Manson, wounded, three men killed
and 25 wounded.

A territorial battalion takes these losses much more
to heart than a regular unit, The men of each com-

18

pany are mainly drawn from the same district or village, there are brothers and cousins side by side, while there is also the intimate friendship which springs from association together since boyhood. One can scarcely realize the sadness of a trench burial in a battalion such as ours.

Picture one such scene vividly fixed in our memories. Here, immediately behind the front line, is a great shell-hole. The bottom of this was deepened slightly, and the body, wrapped in its blanket, was reverently laid in it, while the shells whined overhead, and the varied noises of battle went on.

A number of officers and men from the neighbouring trench gathered round, while Captain Milligan read those pathetic and glorious passages from the Book of Books, "Man that is born of woman," "I am the resurrection and the life," while all uncovered and some wept.

They then covered over all that was mortal of their comrade and returned to the post of duty, still more steeled against the cold calculating enemy who has brought this bloody conflict on a peaceful country.

On 14th June the battalion was again in the line, preparatory to a renewed attack on the German lines, the purpose being the straightening of the salient from the Orchard southward, as owing to the awkward form of our front line here we were losing heavily day after day.

In our Division, the main attack was made by the 153rd and 154th Brigades, while the 152nd Brigade held the remainder of the Divisional front, with the exception of the Fifth Seaforths who were to advance and connect up between the advancing brigades in their new positions, and the rest of the 152nd Brigade who were to continue to hold the original front.

In the afternoon our artillery opened fire on the German wire and trenches with every available gun, and for some hours the din was terrific, while great clouds of smoke, yellow, black, and light-coloured, rose from the German position.

At 6 p.m. the firing ceased, and the infantry went over in open order, to cross the four or five hundred yards between them and the enemy. In the light of later warfare one can visualize the scene, a grassy plain on a beautiful summer afternoon, no artillery barrage, no proper cutting of the enemy's wire, no firing on his batteries after the infantry started, the infantry advancing absolutely unprotected except by the rifle and machine-gun fire of their comrades, and machine guns were few and far between in those days, and can one wonder that, in spite of heroic efforts, the attack was a failure, and although some got into the enemy trenches they were so few in number that, during the darkness, they had to crawl back to our own line as best they could?

Many a hard lesson had to be learned before we

evolved a system which developed the attack with a chance of success, by a great addition to our gun power, and a greater supply of shells than the miserably inadequate supply we had at that time.

The Fifth Seaforths suffered heavily in proportion to the numbers actually involved in the advance. " C " Company was the first to top the parapet, and this they did in gallant style, advancing under a murderous fire in open order as steadily as if on parade They were horrified to find that on their front the German wire was absolutely intact, and all the survivors could do was to take advantage of any depression in the ground and wait for night.

At 4.30 a.m. a second attack was ordered, but, news having arrived that the 153rd and 154th Brigades had had to retire, the order was countermanded.

On taking the toll of battle, it was found that Lieuts. J. D. L. Mowat and D. Dunnet were killed, and Captains Robertson and Ritson and Lieutenants W. A. Macdonald, E. Fraser, and W. Mowat wounded, while 32 men were killed and 70 wounded.

Many deeds of heroism were performed on that June morning, stretcher-bearers going out and bringing in the wounded under heavy fire. One of the battalion wits, Jockles to name, was lying badly wounded when a rescuer crawled out to him, and after binding up his wounds tried to get him on his back. Jockles, knowing his own avoirdupois, protested, but without avail, for the rescuer lying face downward, pushed himself feet first under Jockles' helpless body until he had him on his back. Then telling him to hold on as well as he could, and exhorting him by saying, " You'll see Kinnairdie yet, Jockles," he crawled on his hands and knees through the long grass until he got to the parapet, where willing hands helped him over. For their gallant rescue work, four of the battalion were subsequently singled out for a distinction, these being Regtl.-Sergt.-Major Don Sutherland, the D.C.M. and Croix de Guerre, Coy.-Sergt.-Major Jim Bruce, Cpl. John Duchart and Drummer Bocock the D.C.M.

When one compares the elaborate signalling arrangements made prior to an attack in 1917 or 1918, and thinks of the numerous telephone cables buried 6 feet deep, with elaborate dug-outs at cableheads, and all the numerous switchboards, ring telephones, etc., used, the very rudimentary apparatus and cable used in this attack provoke a smile.

There were no buried cables, simply thin insulated wires laid along the top of the communication trench, with one or two alternative routes laid across the fields and carried across roads, on trees, or ruined houses, with the result that, as soon as the German artillery retaliated, all communication between the front line and battalion headquarters and between that and brigade forward headquarters was cut, the lines being in many places blown to pieces.

The experience of two signallers in attempting to restore communication, and, failing that, in bringing back information as runners is worthy of description.

Setting off from headquarters along one of their field lines, they ran the wire through their hands to find any fault or break. They got on all right until about 200 yards from the front trench, when they found it utterly impossible to go further, as shell after shell was dropping on and around a ruined house in front, where the wire was fastened.

They took refuge in an old German trench, and put on their instrument to see if they could get into touch with their rear station, which they did. During the progress of this work every shell explosion sent clods of earth and scraps of iron over their heads, one shell striking so near that the entire trench trembled and shook.

Finding it futile to go further, they ran the gauntlet across country to a communication trench 300 yards away, arriving there just in time to receive the sad news of the deaths of Lieuts. Mowat and Dunnet and the hold-up of the attack, with which news they hurried back to headquarters.

At midnight these two lads set off again to repair the line under cover of darkness, and to save floundering over ditches (many, 6 feet wide and 9 or 10 feet deep), they cycled round by a main road, through Festubert, which passed the house referred to above

WAR DIARY OF THE FIFTH SEAFORTHS

On arriving here they found, as they expected, that their wire was broken where it crossed the road ; but, search and grope as they would, no trace of the other end could they find. Thinking they were well back behind our lines, they, for a second, flashed an electric torch on the wire, and in a minute the German machine-gun bullets were smack into the back of the building, although not one had been heard before. Then shells started to hop around, and they crawled into a half-ruined sand-bag shelter beside the house to wait for a lull in the hailstorm. Into this shelter in a few minutes darted two R.G.A. men, coming from the trenches for provisions, who had run the gauntlet for 300 yards.

As the early dawn was now faintly showing, and detection would be still easier by daylight, one of the party crossed the road on hands and knees, and then went bounding over the everlasting ditches into a field of corn (natural growth), all heavy with dew, to get the wire. There were, however, so many wires at this part, all broken and seemingly leading the same way, that the attempt had to be abandoned in despair.

The men then made a sprint along the shell-pitted road for the shelter of the communication trench, crouching low and lying flat when the German flares lit up the country around.

Floundering into the trench, they met another party, also out repairing wires, this time along the trench, and one of them went up to the firing-line to get further news of the day's casualties. He found our men lining the parapet, blazing away every now and again at anything stirring in the German lines, and even at the top of the trench to make them keep their heads down and allow " B " Company to go out in greater security beyond the trench, and also to protect the stretcher-bearers carrying back the wounded to the Aid Posts at the rear.

These stretcher-bearers, many of them pipers and drummers of the battalion, are plucky fellows, for they go out to the front without the excitement of the attack to stimulate them, and have to come slowly back carrying the wounded, and so cannot drop when they hear a shell coming, but can only hope it is going somewhere else.

Well, now for the adventures of our two linesmen. At 3 a.m. a slight haze was on, just before sunrise, so they resolved to have another try at the wire, and returned once more to the ruined house. One remained there, while the other, carrying a drum of wire, made a wide detour across country to the rear, and came in at a part where he knew he would find his wire.

After losing his way in the maze of trenches, ditches, etc., he at length found it, and ran along it until it came to an end on the edge of a great 15-feet wide crater excavated by a shell. Here he joined on his new wire on the drum, the old wire beyond having disappeared, and quickly retraced his way to the house.

Their old friend, the machine gunner, apparently again noticed some movement, for the crack of his bullets on the brick began once more, and when one of the lads went to tie up the wire in a tree a bullet entered the trunk a few inches over his head.

Now the instrument was put on, and having got in touch with the front trenches and headquarters, the two brave lads shouted " Hurrah," and resolved to make a run for their bicycles which were a quarter of a mile away. For the first hundred yards or so the road lay open, and they painfully thought of the machine gunner's ever vigilant eye. It had to be done, however, as the mist was getting dissipated by the morning sun, and, providentially, at that moment a big " Jack Johnson " (the fellows that throw up a cloud of black smoke) struck the road 10 yards away, and the dense smoke floated back towards the supposed position of the gunner. With a " now for it," off they bolted into the cloud, and though the gunner spied them beyond it, and sent a few shots after them, they had now their sprinting speed on, and were going further away every minute.

On coming to their bicycles, they found 78 men formed up, all that had so far come back belonging to the Liverpool Irish which had attacked the Germans on the previous night at least 800 strong. Of course many stragglers would rejoin later, but still it gives one the idea of what modern unsuccessful attack means in losses.

LAVENTIE SECTOR, JULY 1915

On the night of 23rd June the much needed relief of the Division took place, and the battalion went into billets at West La Coutoure, a most beautiful spot where the men were billeted in farms embowered among the trees. Here twelve days' rest was expected, but on the 25th we moved to La Gorgue and by the 27th we were in the trenches in front of Laventie, a little to the north of Neuve Chapelle.

Here we found a nice peaceful sector where apparently the " gentlemen over the way " were Saxons, for on one occasion they shouted over, " We Saxons, you Anglo-Saxons, don't shoot," and on their being relieved a few days later they shouted to our men that Prussians were relieving them, and asked us to give them hell, showing the nice brotherly feeling existing between Prussian and Saxon.

In this Sector, we had our first experience of mining, for on the night of the 30th our tunnellers exploded a mine under the German front line trench, which blew about 30 or 40 yards of it into the air. A dense cloud of smoke, earth, beams, etc., rose into the air. The ground shook, a muffled roar was heard, and then with a crash all our artillery and machine guns opened out with rapid for 10 or 20 minutes, hoping to catch the Boche in the open as he would naturally expect an attack in the gap in his line.

In this area we remained until 26th July, during which time our total casualties were six killed and five wounded, so that on the whole this month was regarded by the battalion rather in the light of a picnic.

Some of the tricks played by our men on the Boche are really good.

One platoon faked up a good Highlander the other morning, with Balmoral bonnet, tunic, etc., who bravely exposed himself over the parapet, drawing a tremendous lot of fire from the Germans, who must have thought either that they were beastly poor shots or that the Scottie opposite must have had a charmed life. Then when a shot strikes the parapet our boys signal back an " inner," " magpie," etc., with a spade or a " miss " with any old rag stuck on a stick. That invariably brings two or three more in rapid succession, but the parapet is thick and no harm is done.

The other night a melancholy voice was heard in no-man's land between them and us shouting for help —a German ruse to play on our inherently soft and sympathetic natures ; but, no fear. The gentle voice got rapid fire for two or three minutes and then the same voice shouted " D——d Scotties " in quite a different tone !

Some good stories have been going the round of late.

28

An Argyll battalion shortly after going into the trenches was greeted by a cornet soloist in the German trenches playing " Bonnie Mary of Argyle," so when the battalion's spell was up their Colonel marched them out of the trenches with his full pipe-band playing " The Campbells are coming," and the Germans were so tickled that they forgot to fire.

We recently got among us a fresh batch from home to be trained in trench warfare. One of these in his virgin greenness and self-conceit raised the ire of some members of a rather tough lot of Paisley Highlanders by referring to them as " Blooming Territorials," so they promptly hoisted him over the top of the parapet and kept him out there for two hours among the barbed wire until he was in rather a shivering condition. Then they said, " Now, if you like, you can come back among the blooming Territorials!" Which he thankfully did.

On 2nd July while in the line near Fauquissart the Company Officers held a little birthday party, this being the natal day of the junior Major commonly known as " Faither " to the various officers who have come under his paternal jurisdiction and sound advice. These officers resolved that war or no war his birthday should be fittingly celebrated, so at 6 p.m. behold us all wending our way to the rather dilapidated farm where the worthy Major and his juniors at present reside.

A sumptuous tea was provided for the occasion by our host, but as the number who had invited themselves greatly augmented the number of *bona fide* guests there were not enough enamelled " moogies " to go round. So a relay system had to be adopted, which rather upset arrangements. The *pièce de résistance* —a tin of sardines—was unfortunately finished by the first contingent (a box of sardines does not go far among fourteen hungry Hielanders !) and the second lot had perforce to content themselves with biscuits and a splendid, nay gorgeous, iced cake, specially sent for the occasion, suitably inscribed with the motto, " Victory, and many happy returns of the day." There was a dessert of red currants, gathered, I expect, from the deserted orchards roundabout.

Thereafter, as chair accommodation was scanty even with the addition of the bed, the party adjourned to the lawn, and, while enjoying the pleasures of My Lady Nicotine in the warm glow of the setting sun, they compared notes with some of the guests recently arrived from Scotland.

As evening fell a return was made to the dining-room, the curtains—an old mat—were drawn, and, in spite of French prohibition and other difficulties, our worthy host managed to produce enough of Scotia's national beverage to enable the company to drink his health suitably, the eldest son providing, as the result of a cycle raid on places further to the rear, a supply of red and white wine for those who appreciate milder beverages.

The eldest son (Captain D. Sutherland) then proposed the toast, " Many happy returns of the day," and referred to the kindly feeling that always existed between their host and his subalterns and men.

This toast had also to be pledged in relays in the same " moogies " that had served as teacups. " For he's a jolly good fellow " was heartily sung, and so lustily that I am afraid the *Tageblatt Zeitung* will have references to-morrow to " Singing and cheering in the British lines near Laventie," and speculations as to the cause thereof.

ALBERT SECTOR, AUGUST 1915

On the night of 26th July the battalion entrained at La Gorgue and, by a most circuitous route via Calais, arrived at Corbie on the 27th and marched to a pretty little village called Pont Noyelle on the Amiens-Albert road.

On the 30th a move was made by road to Martinsart, a rather battered village slightly north of Albert, so famous for its ruined cathedral. This noble church, with its magnificent tower surmounted by a golden statue of the Virgin and Child, was too splendid a target for the Boche, and the great figure, 20 feet in height, now hangs head downward from the top of the tower, the Infant Saviour with His hands outstretched over the shattered town as if invoking a blessing on the inhabitants in their time of danger and distress.

Here we heard the prophecy that, when the statue fell, the power of Germany would come to an end, and in 1918 we saw its accomplishment, for although strengthened with iron bars and beams by British engineers in 1917 to prevent its fall, yet when the German arms, in what they considered their final and victorious advance of March 1918, recaptured Albert, the artillery duel brought the statue to the ground, and from that moment the German power waned, and their last hope of victory was extinguished.

We took over this sector from the 116th French Infantry Regiment, who had held it for some considerable time, and who fought very gallantly in the French Champagne offensive a month later.

The taking-over was much more difficult than taking-over from a British unit, not only the language difficulty causing confusion, but French ideas as to trenches, dug-outs, rules of the game, etc., were very different from ours, and we took some time to rearrange things to our mind.

The country in this sector is very different from the other parts of France we have been in. We had so far been accustomed to perfectly level roads—not a hill to climb when cycling or riding, nothing but a level horizon as far as one could see. But here the country is a rolling one, with rounded rises or hills up to 160 metres (about 500 feet), dropping down to valleys only 60 metres, or 180 feet above sea-level, and then rising again to similar heights. Trees are everywhere, and there are large woods, consisting of a number of very large trees with thickets of smaller trees about 12 or 15 feet high in between.

Taking over the line, our men are now in the ruined village of Authuille, nicely ensconced in the beautiful valley of the Ancre.

Down this valley flows a nice little river where the water is clear and pure and the current can actually be seen, so different from the sluggish rivers of muddy, dirty water further north. In some places this river, owing to inattention to its banks since the war began, has overflowed and formed large shallows among the trees which surround its course.

Running parallel to the river is a railway, now disused, as it runs straight up the valley into the Boche lines, and has had to be barricaded by our men. On each side there rise fairly steep slopes, and on the eastern slope stands our village, pretty well shattered but with some houses still habitable. The rest of the battalion is disposed of in shelters of wood, corrugated iron, and clay in the valley near the railway, and on the side of the slope, where they are quite sheltered, or nearly so, from shell-fire through the steepness of the hill-side. Above them are the trenches, looking in the distance like so many zig-zag, ugly white scars on the beautiful scene. These trenches were made by the French.

The dug-outs here are marvellous. Fancy a small opening in the ground, and looking down you see a 12-foot ladder, on descending which you come to a large room cut out of the solid chalk, with generally primitive beds of a framework of branches with wire-netting nailed on them (although some sybarites had carried wooden or iron bedsteads from the ruined houses, and even hung up pictures on the walls). In some of these dug-outs, there is, leading from the first floor, another opening and ladder going further down still, where you find a second chalk cavern underneath the first ; and, I am told, there are one or two of three-story depth.

The Boche is quite near—in some places only 60 or 70 yards separating the two lines of trenches. On the whole, the line is a very quiet one, and there is not much shelling or even rifle fire.

" Faither " has made a great " find " in his new villa. (No, it was not even white or red wine—the French had been here ten months, remember.) A swarm of bees had made a nest between the tiles and the ceiling, and some of the more venturesome youngsters of the " family " had, at the expense of swollen hands and faces, attacked the bees and brought down some great slabs of delicious honeycomb, and with it and some other delicacies a very nice tea was set out, to which we all did justice.

The river is a great attraction here ; not for boating,

although Gerry volunteered to give me a cruise in an ancient-looking boat which still survives the vicissitudes of war. Every afternoon hundreds of the fellows may be seen bathing in the river, and thankfully enjoying so good an opportunity of getting rid of some of the dust and grime of the campaign.

On 14th August the battalion was relieved by the Indian Cavalry Division and went back to rest billets at Buire where it remained until the 21st.

The fleas in this village are of a particularly healthy and vigorous type. We had selected one nice, clean-looking brick-built barn, well floored with fresh-looking straw, but in reality as whited a sepulchre as ever we met with. Four stalwart military policemen, each at least 6 feet 2 inches in height, took possession of this barn and threw themselves on the straw with a sigh of relief.

Within half an hour these policemen were utterly routed and fled from the barn vowing that wild horses would not drag them back to it. So fierce was the onslaught and so innumerable were the hordes of the enemy that it was impossible to withstand the attackers, who advanced, front, flank, and rear, and gave no chance of successfully withstanding them.

Since then, however, a Trench Mortar Battery has taken possession, and perhaps with different weapons they may manage to make a good fight of it, but I still await the result with considerable dubiety.

Later.—The Battery people were also routed!

On the 21st the battalion took over the trenches in front of Becourt from the 7th Gordons. Becourt Château, the battalion headquarters, was once a splendid mansion-house embowered in lofty trees, and, although perched high above the trench line which here runs along the bottom of the valley towards that scene of death and devastation called La Boiselle, once a pretty village but now a charnel house, yet it has survived months of shelling wonderfully well and, although bearing a few honourable scars in roof and wall, it is still habitable in the military sense.

Attached to the château is a little private chapel in which the altar and statue still stand although shells have pierced the walls. A pair of swallows have built their nests above the altar, and it was very interesting to see the parent birds flying out and in, settling for a moment on the cross and then sweeping round towards the nest with a little chirp, at which the heads of the fledglings with gaping beaks at once protruded. It reminded one very forcibly, in midst of these terrible scenes, of that old psalm, written by a doughty warrior of long ago :

> "The swallow also for herself hath 'stablished a nest,
> Even thine own altars, where she safe
> Her young ones forth may bring."

And true enough the old psalm seemed here. Beneath the chapel were the family vaults, with recesses for the departed of the Becourt family, and being deep dug and safe our fellows had no scruple at night-time in retiring into its dark depths, and, wrapped in their blankets, slumbering peacefully in those recesses until daylight or duty once again brought them to the surface.

This château was formerly the residence of a Count, and is a splendid example of Boche methods of pillage. In their retiral, early in the war, they held it for a few days, and in that time their search was crude but thorough. Take one room as an example, a bedroom belonging to one of the ladies of the house. Going in, one stepped into a sea of ladies' clothes, two or three feet deep, dresses, underclothes, hats, etc., scattered over the floor. The lovely wardrobes, chests of drawers and wall cupboards had been ruthlessly smashed open, the beautifully carved woodwork being splintered and broken, while everything of value had been removed.

The British and German trenches in the vicinity of La Boiselle are in some places only 10 yards apart, and to speak above a whisper brings over a hand grenade from the watchful Boche, while, the chalky ground being admirably adapted for tunnelling, the digging and exploding of mines under each other's front lines is the order of the day, and one never knows when the ground may heave and rise under one's feet, hurling all in the vicinity to destruction.

It was of this sector that the battalion poet, the late

WAR DIARY OF THE FIFTH SEAFORTHS

Lieut. E. A. Mackintosh, M.C., wrote in his book *War, the Liberator*:

What are you doing, Sentry,
Fresh-faced and brown?
Waiting for the mines, Sir.
Sitting on the mines, Sir,
Just to keep them down.
Mines going up, and no one to tell for us,
Where it will be, and may be it's as well for us,
Mines going up, Oh! God, but it's hell for us,
Here with the bloody mines.

Where are you lying, Sentry?
Wasn't this your place?
Down below your feet, Sir.
Below your heavy feet, Sir,
With earth upon my face.
Mines gone up, and the earth and clod on us—
Fighting for breath—and our own comrades trod on us,
Mines gone up—Have pity, oh God! on us,
Down in the bloody mines.

On 2nd September the battalion went into rest billets after its spell of trench duty, at Henencourt, a nice village two miles north of the Albert-Amiens road. Rest to a battalion near the line is rather a euphemistic term, for it implies fatigue parties of from 200 to 500 every night walking 5 or 6 miles to the trenches, digging new trenches, repairing old, or carrying ammunition for 5 or 6 hours, and then trudging back again about 6 or 7 a.m. utterly wearied and exhausted. However, there were clean barns and stables, and for the lucky ones dwelling-houses instead of firesteps and crowded dug-outs, and there were also the village *estaminets* in the evening for gossip, beer, wine, and a smoke, and with that they were content.

Here it was that the sergeants of "B" Company resolved to form a Sergeants' Mess for which they hired a room in a village farm. So successful was the venture, that the opening ceremony took place with great éclat four nights in succession. On the fourth, the greatest and final night, it was resolved to send for Sergt. Mackay, the battalion Harry Lauder, to cheer the company with his inimitable songs.

Sergt. Mackay at the time was attached to the Medical Officer, and a scout reported that he was asleep in the medical orderly room at the extreme end of the village. As his bed consisted of an army stretcher, it was resolved to fetch him asleep or awake, so two of the most stalwart members of the mess were despatched, and soon appeared after bringing him through the streets, and deposited him, stretcher and all, on the mess-room floor.

A little liquid refreshment having been gently administered, the redoubtable William thereafter arose and regaled the company with song and story until the " wee sma' hours."

On 11th September our happy time ended, and once again we did the dreary round of La Boiselle, with its mines, trench mortars, and shells, but on the 18th we were once more back at Henencourt, where on the 21st the battalion was inspected by Lord Kitchener. At the close of the inspection, turning to Col. Davidson, the famous Field-Marshal said, " Well, Colonel, you have the finest body of men I have ever seen," and from such an authority that was the highest praise a battalion could get.

After the inspection the battalion marched to the trenches, taking up a new sector slightly north of the last, in front of Aveluy, a village on the Ancre to the north of Albert.

Here our trenches were on the edge of a large wood of magnificent trees which had not as yet suffered much from artillery fire. Further back in the wood were the support and reserve line trenches with dug-outs and shelters where the men were quite comfortable. During this period the weather was very broken, with thunderstorms and heavy downpours of rain, and one company on trench digging fatigue, fertile in ideas and full of resource, before leaving their dug-outs, put off all their clothing except their boots and kilt aprons, and, thus lightly clad, they dug and shovelled for five or six hours, while the rain fell in torrents. On coming off parade, this wise company hung their kilt aprons out of doors, gave themselves a good rub down, donned their nice warm underclothing and went to bed, while the other poor unfortunates had either to search for dry underclothes or shiver in their wet garments.

On 26th September we again returned to Henencourt where we saw our first aeroplane duel, which, although we have seen many since, remains vividly impressed on our memories as being the first. At 8 a.m. a German aeroplane came across to spy out the land, and passed over our village.

The anti-aircraft guns were soon cracking away, and the white puffs of the shells were all around, but seemingly doing no harm.

Catching sight of a British aeroplane the German airman started to pursue it, when suddenly, out of a fleecy white cloud higher up, there swooped downward like a bolt from heaven, another British plane which had been scouting over the German lines and was now returning.

Then began a battle royal. The anti-aircraft guns ceased for fear of injuring our own plane, and the two giant " birds " began circling round each other, the British plane sometimes rushing close in, then wheeling away again, while all the time their machine guns were firing rapidly.

Suddenly a " Hurrah " went up from our little group of spectators, for the German suddenly dropped with a terribly steep twisting dive just like a bird with a broken wing.

After falling a thousand feet or more, it straightened out for a second or two, as if the aeronaut had made a frantic effort to regain control.

The Briton, when his opponent dropped, followed

him in graceful spiral curves, and, when he righted, recommenced firing at him. Then came two bursts of white smoke when apparently a bullet exploded the petrol tank. The wings, till then standing straight out, doubled up as if closing above the body, and with the engine making a weird, pathetic, throbbing sound, down dived the plane to the ground like a stone.

On going to the spot what a scene of ruin! The heavy four-cylinder engine was embedded in the ground, the wings and body were mostly shattered splinters of wood scattered all around, the steel stays were bent and twisted, and the two airmen lay dead.

On examination, one had several bullets through head and wrist, while the other's body was perforated with bullets, showing the deadly accurate fire of our airman.

On 30th September the battalion was back once more in the Authuille sector, where in August we had such happy times.

Here we are under the shadow of the mighty German fortress of Thiepval, which frowns down upon our happy valley and lets us know of its predominating position by its frequent outbursts of trench mortar and artillery fire. During October, November, and December we alternated between trench duty and rest billets, holding the Authuille or Aveluy sectors, and resting either in Henencourt or Bouzincourt. The weather broke early, and November and December were noted for their spells of hard frost, followed by dreary days of cold, drenching rain, which brought down our laboriously-built trenches in a mass of clay and water, covering the duckboards 3 or 4 feet deep under the filthiest, stickiest, most abominable mud that man ever tried to drag his weary legs through.

Rats were the bane of our lives in this area, and if ever there was a place infested with rats it was Authuille and the trenches in front of it, and if ever there was need for the " Pied Piper of Hamelin " to charm them into the neighbouring river it was here. Wherever you go you hear them squeaking or settling family quarrels. When you fall off to sleep they come frolicking around, run over your body or face, and generally give you the " jumps," completely banishing the sweet influence of Morpheus. A man when lying sleeping in a dug-out fully clothed has been known to find one up under his tunic, and they are such a nuisance that war is waged upon them wherever and whenever possible.

One worthy officer hailing not far from Kildonan is particularly noted for unfailing accuracy with his trusty stick, and last night he marshalled three or four others, and with two electric torches and good hefty sticks they sallied out. Woe to the unfortunate rat which had selected the same hour for his nightly peregrination, for he never returned to his domicile ! Dazzled by the brightness of the torch, he was utterly nonplussed as to the direction to make for safety, and down came the unerring stick, and with a squeak his career of theft and mischief came to an end. A good dozen were accounted for, the major portion of the bag falling to the aforesaid officer, who retired for the night with the consciousness of having earned a good night's repose.

The evenings were now getting longer and colder, and in rest billets the monotony of the dark nights was relieved by battalion concerts held in a large hall at Henencourt château, where Lieut. E. A. Mackintosh cheered us with his own songs, such as " The Smoke Helmet," " The A.S.C.," " Four and twenty Bombers," etc., while Sergt. Mackay gave us the real " Harry Lauder " touch with " Hey, Donald ! " " The Lass of Tobermory," and " When the Wedding Bells are Ringing." As showing how difficult it is for the officer fresh from home to appreciate the conditions out here, an experience with a newly-arrived subaltern might be related. He rolled up to headquarters at Henencourt one evening under orders to report that night at Authuille.

Imagine the mirth of the orderly officer when the callow youth calmly asked him :

" Is there an hotel at Authuille where I can put up for the night until I find my unit ? "

" Oh, yes," said the officer, " you can go to the Hotel de Authuille, noted for its light airy rooms, no windows or doors, its spring-mattressed beds, branches, and rabbit wire-netting, its ample and satisfying cuisine, bully and dog biscuits, and its early morning gong for sleepy guests, the Boche Strafe at 5 a.m."

On realizing the charms of this hotel, he plaintively said, " Can't I stay here for the night and go down in the morning ? " but the fates (in this case, General Ross) were inexorable, and down he had to go.

With the approach of winter the transport men's difficulties have begun in earnest. It is bad enough to lead or drive your heavily-laden waggons along good roads on a black night, but when you have to leave roads and trust to cross-country tracks full of ruts and holes which take the horses to the knees, when you have to feel rather than see your way, and when these difficulties are aggravated by the whine of the machine-gun bullet, the crash of the shell, or the smash of the minenwerfer bomb, then the life of the transport driver is no sinecure, envied although he was by one and all during the summer months.

We now come to the story of the irrepressible female.

In the shattered town of Albert a young lady appeared one afternoon on a push-bike and gallantly headed up the broad main road, at the top of which was the entrance to our communication trenches. Here the sentry stopped her, and she was escorted back to the Town Marshal, the officer who acts the part of chief constable of the town. On questioning her, he found that she was no spy, but one of those journalistic ladies, eager for something original for her paper—such as " A lady journalist's visit to the trenches "—and who had cajoled the Mayor of the chief town further back to give her a pass or permit to this town.

The Town Marshal gave her twenty-four hours to clear out, but, instead of doing so, she next exercised her blandishments over a friendly sapper, who provided her with a suit of uniform and an empty cellar as a residence. And there she spent six or seven days, until some one again informed the officer.

She was then locked in an upper room, and the Provost Marshal (the chief police official of the Division) was sent for to escort the prisoner to headquarters. This official rode over, but picture the mirth of his brother-officers when he arrived back leading the horse, with his prisoner, still in uniform, calmly surveying the situation from the saddle of his mount !

Brought before the General (" and a stern old man was he "), she took matters just as coolly, and when asked in a severely magisterial fashion, " Young woman, do you realize you could be shot for what you have done ? " she nonchalantly replied, " Quite so, quite so."

On leaving the room after getting a terrific lecture she turned round, sweetly smiling, and, with a little

wave of the hand to the General, said, " Ta-ta, ta-ta,"
leaving him in a speechless condition.

Attached to Brigade headquarters just now there
is a Field Company private, Beverley to name, who
is a mighty souvenir hunter. Beverley, finding an
unexploded German shell one day, and wishing to get
it emptied in order to send the case to his mother,
tucked it under his arm and marched into an artillery
dug-out, as being the most likely place to find experts
in this line. The three occupants at once fled outside
(an unexploded shell is at best a very dangerous toy),
and, standing fifty yards away, ordered Beverley to
clear out, as they had no desire to be blown sky-high.

Beverley reluctantly departed with his prize, and,
loath to part with it, but finding it heavy, he tied a
rope to it and went up the hill dragging it behind him !
On the top of the rise stood a lieutenant who, on seeing
what Beverley was pulling along, held up his hands
in horror and shouted, " Stop, stop, you madman !
Do you wish to commit suicide ? "

So poor Beverley had to leave his prize. But next
day, finding an equally foolhardy chum, the two went
back and managed to remove the fuse and empty out
the explosive without any accident.

As showing how even the animal creation learns to
dodge shells, an incident occurred at Martinsart which
is worth relating.

Six shells fell into the courtyard of a farm one afternoon. Three cows were standing together in the yard, and when they heard the ominous whistle of the first shell coming near all three lay down; in such a hurry, in fact, that they bumped into each other in doing so. The six shells came in quick succession, and the cows lay quite still until a lull came after the sixth, when they jumped up, bolted as hard as they could in different directions, and took cover in some of the buildings.

Then the famous cow of the 6th Seaforths, which has all the summer supplied a goodly quantity of milk to that battalion, and which had a special dug-out built for her in the wood, in addition to the honour of being entered as one of the trench stores to be handed over to the incoming battalion, was a wary, old, sagacious " bird." She was led down every day to graze in the valley, but one day a few bullets went over her head, so she turned, pulled the rope out of her attendant's hand, bolted for her dug-out, and absolutely refused to stir abroad for some hours after.

How " A " Company's boys got no sugar in their tea is rather an interesting reminiscence of our stay in the happy valley with its ruined village, its river, and surrounding swamps. To cross the swamp from the village to the railway where at the time " A " Company were living in dug-outs along the line, the " Fifth " had made a road composed of sticks and brushwood laid on the swampy ground, this foundation being covered with a thick coating of broken brick and chalk, with bridges of tree trunks where the deepest channels lay. This road was utterly unprotected with side-rails, and a false step in the dark landed you into a marsh, varying from 3 feet to 8 or 9 feet in depth. Having stayed rather late one evening in " Faither's " ruined cottage, with its sand-bagged walls, I foolishly resolved to take this road as being my shortest way to my bike, and so to Headquarters. But I speedily repented, for the night was as dark as tar and I had no electric torch to keep my footsteps on the narrow path. However, every now and then, a German flare light rose in the air over the crest of the valley, making everything as light as day for a few seconds, and then it was a case of sprinting along the track and halting when a still deeper darkness fell on the scene.

I had just got half-way across when the confounded Germans ran out of flares or got tired of wasting them, and I was stuck. Suddenly I heard cheery voices coming behind, and in a few minutes three forms appeared, stepping merrily out, as if they had cats' eyes. I swung in behind them and was admiring their confidence on the narrow way, when a splash and a gasping cry, " Give me your hand," varied the march a little. The road had narrowed at a deeper part to form a bridge and No. 1 had walked straight into 9 or 10 feet of water. However, we grabbed his wrists, and when we did so he became more anxious about three sand-bags he was carrying in his left hand, and which had also gone overboard with him when he fell. We hauled the sand-bags, as we thought, on to terra firma, and then the man, but lo, and behold ! when we looked for the sand-bags only two could we find, and although we lay on our stomachs and lit matches so as to peer into the marsh, the bag had been so completely swallowed up that no trace of it could be seen. On examining, by gentle pressure, the other two, the soaked soldier in a sad voice announced, " It's ' A ' Company's sugar; their tea won't be very sweet to-morrow, I'm afraid ! "

During December the battalion had in hand the initiation into trench warfare of a unit of the new army just arrived in France, the method being to take them in among the old companies by platoon, by half company and by company, until finally the new battalion relieved the old.

As an illustration of taking the drill book too literally, and rigidly following out its conditions under all circumstances, the men of the new battalion here afforded a good example the other day. The drill book says that on hearing a shell coming every man is to throw himself flat on the ground in order to have a better chance of escaping flying splinters, etc. A platoon of new-comers was in a particularly muddy part of the firing-line, when the Germans sent a few shells over, and every man promptly flopped on his stomach in the bottom of the trench, sending a wave of mud out on each side of him. One can picture their condition thereafter, and understand that next time a shell comes over they will forget drill book precepts and, applying common-sense ones, plaster themselves as flat as they can against the side of the trench instead of getting plastered in the bottom of it.

At Christmas the battalion was at Bouzincourt and one fine afternoon the Colonel ordered all the officers to parade for a ride to Henencourt, the transport officer having promised to provide mounts of some type for all.

The ride can best be described in the words of Lieut. E. A. Mackintosh, M.C., the bombing officer of the battalion.

We arrived at the starting-point and there was a horrible lot of horses, all looking excessively wild. In fear and trembling I approached Sergt. Mackenzie, and he pointed out as my mount a small black pony about the size of a respectable collie dog. The animal looked at me on my approach and burst into a fit of uncontrollable laughter. Sergt. Mackenzie, lengthening the stirrups until they almost touched the ground, wedged my feet, which are popularly supposed to be the largest in France to-day, into the smallest stirrup irons I have ever seen. The groom let go of the bridle, and I said to Keston (the other beginner), who was mounted on an enormous but exceedingly docile animal with a

51

strong resemblance to a camel, " Come on, let's go."
He said, " Wait a minute." But at this point my
horse made up its own mind, and I had only time to
shout, " I'm going," before I found myself painfully
engaged in what I believe is called a canter, after the
rest of the procession.

I drew up alongside the doctor, who told me that
probably my pony wanted to see its sister, on which
he was mounted. I said, " For heaven's sake, get
your beast back." But at that point my horse seemed
to get tired of the family, and rushed up alongside the
Colonel, bumping me in a most unpleasant manner.
The Colonel said, " You're a junior officer ; what are
you doing up here ? " I replied, " I'm not here of my
own free will ; you'll have to talk to the horse, sir ! "

Then Captain Rutherford came alongside of me and
said, " Saw her mouth ; saw her mouth, man ! " So
I asked, " How the devil do you do that ? " And on
his explanation I " sawed," at which the little beast
immediately began to bump up and down underneath
me, and Gid. cried, " Stop sawing, Tosh, she's rearing."
So I stopped, and the next thing I knew, I was away
past Colonel, Major, and all the rest, bumping horribly,
and going extremely fast past the football field. Every
" Fifth " man on the field immediately stopped his
game, lined up, and gave me a tremendous cheer as I
rushed past, to which my only answer was, " Go to
blazes out of this ! "

At this stage of the proceedings I lost my bonnet, but by this time I cared nought about bonnets. We seemed to jolt on for miles, until I began to feel as if I were breaking asunder at the waist, when suddenly " Faither " and Stalk came tearing up behind me. " Turn her into the soft ground," shouted " Faither," and I managed to pull her off the road and head her for a haystack, which looked a comfortable place to fall into.

The little brute, however, was too smart for me, and, spotting the haystack, she turned back into the road over two prodigious heaps of stones which nearly shook my liver out. Stalk passed at this moment, and, seeing a streak of foam from the horse on my face, shouted, " For goodness' sake, stop him, Major, he's foaming at the mouth."

At that point Stalk's horse bolted too, and we had a hammer-and-tongs race up the hill, missing a mess cart coming in the opposite direction by a fraction of an inch. At the top of the hill Stalk pulled up, and I passed him, clinging determinedly to the saddle and praying that my beast would have a heart attack and die on the spot. But no such luck.

The Major shouted, " Speak to her, Tosh." And I tried to say in a cajoling voice, " Woa, lass ; steady, old girl." But she seemed to pay no attention, and it soon became, " Stop, you —— ! " which appeared to spur her to further efforts.

I was just beginning to calculate the mileage I should have to travel, when the Major saw two sappers, and shouted to them, " Stop her ! " They began to jump up and down and scream, which so astonished the pony that she stopped suddenly, nearly shooting me over her head.

Assisted by the R.E. men, I got my feet out of the stirrups, and thanked heaven I was on earth again. When " Faither " arrived he asked me if I was hurt, to which I replied, " I don't feel as if there was any of me left below my breast."

After a bit, quite an assemblage turned up, including the Colonel, who was nearly falling off his horse with laughter. He advised me to lead the horse, to which I replied, " I intend to do so, sir. I would rather bomb a German sap once a week than mount that beast again. But how will I lead her ? " He explained the method, and I departed leading the horse, which appeared to be unable to look at me without laughing.

After dragging the beast along shamefacedly for a couple of miles, I met a groom, also laughing, who took charge of her. Now, when I meet that horse on a route march I cannot look her in the face. Give me a quiet, self-respecting bomb, but no more horses for me !

On 28th December the battalion bade farewell to Henencourt, Aveluy, and Authuille, and marched

south to rest billets in the village of Molliens-au-Bois, a
cheerful little place, where we were soon on good terms
with the inhabitants, and spent six happy weeks,
training hard for what all anticipated would be the
more strenuous work of 1916.

CHAPTER III

THE 1916 CAMPAIGN

MOLLIENS-AU-BOIS

WE brought in the New Year with full Highland honours. When twelve midnight came, the pipers of the battalion formed up outside headquarters and marched through the principal streets of the village, and it was at once manifest from the numbers that turned out of their billets that few, if any, had gone to bed before the mystic hour that ushers in the New Year. Each barn had its own little sing-song, each Sergeants' Mess was also very much alive, while all the officers of the battalion, on the Colonel's invitation, were present at a dinner at headquarters, which in the present instance is part of the village school. Twenty-two officers sat down to dinner at 7.30, and all the items of the menu reflected great credit on the headquarters' cooks, who simply excelled themselves on this occasion. After the time-honoured toast of " The King " had been proposed and pledged, a most interesting programme of songs and recitations was taken part in and, when midnight came, there were the usual New Year greetings and the fervent hope expressed that New Year's Day, 1917, would be ushered in in the dear homeland, with war a thing of the past.

During the evening various toasts were proposed and honoured, the principal being those of our Brigadier, General Ross of Cromarty; our O.C., Colonel Davidson, and our Second in Command, Major Sinclair. Nor were our " friends at home " forgotten, the toast of their health and happiness being also duly honoured.

On the return of the pipe-band to headquarters about 12.30 a.m. after their march through the village, a crowd of two or three hundred men of the battalion followed them and the Colonel went out and wished them a happy New Year. On the call of one of the men three hearty cheers were given for the Colonel.

At 11 a.m. there was a football match between the officers of the 5th and 6th Seaforths, which the 6th won by 2 goals to 1, although our battalion had decidedly the best of the game. In the afternoon there was a friendly match between teams representing the men of the two battalions, when again the 6th won—this time by 2 goals to nil.

On 3rd January training began in earnest—route marches, squad-drill, attack and defence, bombing, signalling, and machine-gunning each having its own share in the day's work The lecture rooms are generally barns, which have beeen cleared of their accumulation of old straw and refuse of all kinds. Rough seats and desks of planking have been fitted in, the mud walls patched up with straw and mud to lessen draughts, and so you have an up-to-date school complete.

On 22nd January the battalion with deep regret bade farewell to Col. Davidson who had relinquished the Command.

He has been a member of the battalion for the long period of 25 years, and has been Colonel since shortly after mobilization.

The Command has been taken over by Lieut.-Col. Spooner.

On 29th January the battalion marched to Acheux, a town 15 miles further north, where for a week they worked at the construction of a new railway, returning on 5th February.

On 8th February hurried orders came to move to Corbie, one of the larger towns in the Somme valley, where for twelve days the battalion had a delightful change of scene and billet from the smelly farming villages and dirty barns and outhouses which have been their rest billets since coming to France. This was too good to last, and on the 20th the battalion, wearing for the first time the steel helmets afterwards so indispensable a part of the soldier's equipment, went into tents in the Bois des Tailles, a wood betweeen Corbie and Bray, where for a week they were engaged repairing the roads, at this time in a most wretched condition from excessive traffic and neglect.

As frost and snow came at the same time, the Bois des Tailles was not regarded as a particularly ideal spot, especially as a persistent Boche airman, having located the tents, was in the habit of popping across at odd times, dropping a bomb or two and as quickly clearing out again, and the walls of a tent do not engender a feeling of security when aeroplane bombs are dropping.

Fortunately no casualties occurred, although he rather rudely interrupted one or two football matches.

It was at the time intended that we should relieve, at Bray and Suzanne, the Division which formed the right flank of the British front, the French holding the line south of Suzanne, but after one or two battalions taking over, they were suddenly withdrawn on 29th February and once again we marched back to Molliens-au-Bois.

March was ushered in with a heavy snowfall, but on the 6th the Division was on the move north, and the battalion spent the night and next three days in Beauval, a nice, clean village.

Here we learned that the French, who were still holding an isolated sector in the middle of the British front, just to the north of Arras, were to be relieved by British troops, and that the 51st Division was to take

over that part, known in French annals as the Labyrinth, where in 1914 and 1915 some of the fiercest
battles and heaviest slaughter of the war had taken
place. On the evening of the 10th the battalion
marched into Maroeuil, a little village four miles N.E.
of Arras. To the north stood out prominently the
double tower of Mount St. Eloi on the highest elevation
in the district, which, though often a mark for German
gunners, still proudly reared its spires, battered but
commanding, over the battle line of both armies.

To the south-west could be seen the spire and roofs
of Arras, a large industrial town close up to the firing-
line and yet habitable although bearing some of the
marks of war.

THE LABYRINTH—11TH MARCH TO 14TH JULY 1916

On the night of 11th March our battalion took over
the trenches from the French, and, as I sat in my advanced signal dug-out at Ariane just in front of the main
Arras-Souchez road, I could hear from dusk onward
the heavy tramp of men trudging stolidly up the communication trench which ran past my door. In single
file they went, each man laden with pack, rifle,
ammunition, blankets and rations, and by midnight
nearly 3000 men had passed towards the front, and as
an equal number of French had passed down the
traffic was rather congested.

THE 1916 CAMPAIGN

For some time the moon looked down upon the scene, but after her setting, the darkness of the night was relieved only by the occasional light of a star-shell.

Behind me lies the tree-lined causewayed French main road, now utterly deserted by day, when every one uses the great trenches that run beside it, but at night the transport come along it, bringing up supplies of all kinds for those in the line. These stores are dumped where the several communication trenches meet the road, and long before daylight the road is again bare and deserted. Parties of 50 to 100 men come down the trenches to these dumps and carry up their battalion supplies of food, water, ammunition, bombs, barbed wire, stakes, etc.

As an illustration of German espionage, the French told us that, a day or two before our arrival, a notice board was exhibited above the German trenches which read, " The French will be glad the English are coming to take their place."

Our front here is a great, bare, uninteresting, treeless plain, with all over its surface countless lines of dark red clay or white chalk showing the maze of trenches that have been dug since the armies first settled here.

The tide of battle had ebbed and flowed several times in this area, with the result that the district is a veritable graveyard.

A new trench cannot be dug without coming on hastily-buried dead, grisly hands stick out of the sides of the present trenches, while one machine-gun crew, in making a recess for their gun, tried four times before they found a spot clear of bodies.

The soil here, as at Thiepval, is dry, and therefore suited for mining, at which both sides are now very expert, while the flatness of the country lends itself to trench mortar bombing and sniping. In the sniping department we can lay claim to holding the superiority over the Boche every time, for our snipers are the pick of the gamekeepers and gillies of Sutherland and Caithness, men who can draw a bead on anything within a thousand yards.

Dear old Tosh writes about one of the most famous of these, Sergt. Sandy Macdonald of Kildonan who later fell at Beaumont-Hamel, and who was credited with a score of 97 to his unerring rifle :

> Sniper Sandy's slaying Saxon soldiers,
> And Saxon soldiers seldom show but Sandy slays a few.
> And every day the Boches put up little wooden crosses
> In the cemetery for Saxon soldiers Sniper Sandy slew.

As the days go by we find much more vigour and activity here than further south.

There are constant trench mortar duels, for at last the Government is supplying us with something in the trench mortar line, a little better than an old drain pipe, so that we have some chance to retaliate, but shells are still woefully scarce and have to be husbanded most carefully.

THE 1916 CAMPAIGN

When a Brigadier, on his trenches being blown to atoms by heavy artillery fire, asks for retaliation, and is told by the artillery commander covering his front that he cannot have it as he has only five rounds per gun, and they have to do to the end of the week, it shows the desperate position we were in, even in April 1916, after more than eighteen months of war.

Tosh and his squad of bombers are very busy these nights for there are almost nightly patrol encounters in no-man's land, or in attacks on the saps which here extend some distance forward of the front line.

On 11th April and again on 28th April the enemy was very active, blowing up mines under our front line, and then rushing the positions and trying to establish machine-gun posts on the lips of the mine craters thus formed.

After one of these mines went off, a big German N.C.O. came along a sap towards our men, calling out, " Hands up, Englisher." A diminutive bomber, a left-handed thrower, held up his hands, but with a Mills-bomb in his left, and quick as thought he let the German have the 2 lbs. of steel right in the face, felling him to the ground, when he was at once hauled in as a prisoner.

In one night the Boche blew up no less than five mines, completely altering the appearance of our front line trenches, there being yawning craters and mounds of chalk, where the day before there had been well dug and well kept trenches.

After the explosion, he came across in great numbers and a fierce hand-to-hand fight took place with rifle, bayonet, bomb and bludgeon, but he was driven back leaving several dead, and by strenuous work the damage was hurriedly repaired before daybreak, the men digging and working like demons to form roughly-made trenches and barbed wire defences to replace those which had vanished.

For successfully frustrating what was later found to be a determined effort to break through on our front, the Corps Commander sent a special letter of thanks to the battalions of the 152nd Brigade.

On 1st May the battalion was back in rest at Maroeuil, and to celebrate the first anniversary of our arrival in France an open-air concert was held in the grounds, behind the château. Here where the beauty of the gardens is marred by the ugly roofs of shelters and dug-outs, and where several trees had been lopped by shells a few days before, the battalion gathered at 7.30 p.m., the men sitting on the sloping grassy ground, and the singers gathering round the château piano brought outside for the occasion.

Two men of the 6th Seaforths had rather a hair-raising experience one day. One of them was coming up his dug-out stair when he heard the thud of a trench mortar being fired, and then its descending whizz.

He and the " oil-can " landed at the top of the stair simultaneously, he himself avers he met it on the stair but managed to pass it, so he fled round the nearest traverse and waited for the terrific explosion he expected to follow. His chum down below also heard the bomb falling into the trench, and one can imagine his feelings as he heard it bumping from step to step down the stair. He could not flee so he waited for the end, but with the vagaries of all bombs this one did not explode, but came to rest between his bed and the foot of the stair.

His chum above, after a minute's pause, crept back to the top of the stair and shouted down, " Hey, Sandy, are ye there? " " Ay," came the reply. " Weel, there's an ' oil-can ' doon beside ye," as if Sandy could have been ignorant of the presence of an object as big as a ten-gallon drum.

Later that evening, whether from fear of more bombs, or the bad temper of Sandy, he was found with his kit and blankets going along the trench to make his billet, in, of all places, a bomb-store full of trench-mortar bombs and rifle grenades, apparently considering that a safer place than a 30-foot dug-out.

This choice recalls the man who sat on the parapet under heavy fire rather than get his feet wet in the muddy trench.

In a British official report of the 17th May, the following appeared :—

" Last night two raiding parties of the Seaforth Highlanders entered the German trenches north of Roclincourt. Five Germans were killed in their trench and three dug-outs full of Germans were bombed, one being blown up. Our casualties were slight, and the whole of the raiding parties got back to our trenches."

Such is the official description of the raid carried out by our boys—very bald and bare, but giving the facts of the case.

When it was determined to have this raid, a task which implies taking your life into your hands in a very special sense, volunteers were asked for, with the result that, whereas about 40 were wanted, 100 volunteered for the duty. Those selected were trained by Lieut. E. A. Mackintosh and 2nd Lieut. C. E. Mackay, and on the night of the 16th they were formed into two parties under these officers and took up their positions in our forward saps. A little before 8 p.m. our artillery began the show by raining a hail of shells supplemented by trench mortars, directed on each side and behind the area to be raided. To these the Boche vigorously replied, and in a minute or two the place was a screaming inferno of shells and bombs, our front line being heavily swept by their fire. It is computed that in three-quarters of an hour our artillery fired 2000 shells on this small section of the front, so one can picture the din. It was now dusk, and the flashes of the guns, the flame of bursting shrapnel, the pale light of the star-shells, transformed what was a beautifully calm moonlit night into a whirlwind of devastation and death. After this had gone on for twenty minutes or so, the time fixed for the raiders to advance came, and they rushed over the open, crossed the barbed wire and jumped into the German trenches. Here they came upon five dug-outs with their occupants at home, having gone to earth when the bombardment started. Down the entrances of these they hurled their bombs, the first being greeted with yells and curses, some Boches firing up the stairs at them. After four or five bombs had been thrown silence reigned, but as no mine shaft could be found, one sapper placed a big land mine or box of explosives inside one of the dug-outs, set fire to the fuse, and blew the place sky high. All this took less time than it takes to write it, and the party went rushing along the trenches, seven Germans being met and bayoneted or shot. Several of the men were, however, already wounded, some severely, and the party had to carry or drag these along with it as they made for the appointed exit to return to our lines. Here again they had to rush across the open under the German shrapnel and bombs, yet all the wounded were brought in, only one man being left behind, he having died of his wounds after some of his fellows had dragged him out of the trenches on to the German parapet.

The raid was a successful one, and I subjoin the text of a message sent next day to the battalion:

" Corps Commander desires to convey to Officers, N.C.O.'s and men of the 5th Battalion Seaforth High-landers his highest appreciation of their enterprising and successful raid on enemy trenches on evening of 16th."

Our casualties were: Lieut. Mackay wounded, 4 men killed, and 12 wounded, while the enemy casualties were estimated at 60 at least.

A good story is told in connection with this raid. One of the raiders, realizing the uncertainty of human life, especially when on raiding bent, resolved to put his affairs in order prior to setting out, and, among other things, sent cheques to liquidate his debts, in-cluded among which was an item of 8s. 9d. incurred while in the north previous to coming out—a debt which, for various reasons, he had vowed never to pay, and yet he sent a cheque for it as for the others. In the hurry of the moment, and as one would expect of a mind which is more poetic than business-like, he wrote out a cheque for 9s. 8d. instead. Having come safely back from the raid, the first regret he had was that he ever paid the debt, and the second that he paid 11d. more than he ought.

THE 1916 CAMPAIGN

For organizing and carrying out this raid Lieut. Mackintosh received the M.C. and three of the party M.M.'s.

On 25th May the 152nd Brigade was withdrawn from the line for a rest after being for 74 days continuously in the trenches. During that time, our battalion had been 61 days in the trenches and 13 in the village of Maroeuil, which was daily under shellfire.

31st May, however, saw the end of our rest, and we took over a new sector in front of Neuville St. Vaast, relieving the South Lancs and Border Regiments, who had suffered severely here just previously. The preparations for the battle of the Somme had already begun, the Division we were relieving being withdrawn to refit and train, and our Division had to take over and hold a two-Division front.

What a change this entailed upon our kilted men. To prevent the Boche finding out that our Division had extended its front, the units of the 152nd Brigade had their kilts and Balmoral bonnets taken from them and had been fitted out with khaki trousers and field service caps, much to the disgust of the men, who, suspicious of some Sassenach plot to strip them for ever of the kilt, grumbled very much and protested to their officers.

Neuville St. Vaast, standing in the midst of the labyrinth, is a village which will be for ever famous in the annals of the French. This village was a summer resort for the richer people from the bigger towns around, and had a population of 1500, a number of fine houses, and was beautifully embowered in trees. I passed through Festubert about a year ago, but the destruction there was not nearly so complete as here. Not a vestige of a roof can be seen, not a gable or side wall of any house is complete. Everything that still stands is at most a fragment of wall, and most of the houses are only heaps of brick. The trees, fruit and ordinary, are in the same shattered condition. If not lying on the ground, cut down by shells, they are all scarred, bruised, and battered, branches lopped off, and tops shorn away ; in fact, I looked about to see if I could see a perfect tree and could not find one ; a vivid illustration of the terrific storms of bullets, shells, and fragments of shells that have time and again swept over this deserted village. And yet there is a considerable population living in this desolation— probably 500—but they are British soldiers, and live in the cellars, where they are still intact, or in dug-outs constructed by themselves. Walking along a sunken road in this terrible place, for nearly a mile there was practically a continuous line of little crosses on the slopes of the road, sometimes singly, sometimes in twos and threes, and sometimes in clusters of dozens and scores, showing the terrible toll this place has taken from the sons of France. To picture a town at home of 1500 inhabitants wiped out of existence in this fashion, not a house, hotel, church, or hall left standing, the streets simply footpaths among the litter of brick, stone, and timber from the houses, the very paving-stones and setts turned up and scattered by huge shells, would help one to realize what poor France and Belgium have suffered in hundreds of their towns and villages.

June still saw us in the trenches, and such a June, rain day after day, little or no sunshine, and trenches knee deep in mud and water, dug-outs with water pouring down the stairs, and every one grumbling at "Sunny France" and the manner in which she is be-lying her reputation.

However, when July came in, we began to have hopes of a change, for the 60th London Division, newly out, arrived on the scene, and began training in trench warfare under our supervision; and our surmises were correct, for on July 14th the 51st Division was relieved, and the battalion went into rest billets at Acq.

During our four months' spell in this sector, we have still kept the "luck of the Fifth," for our total casualties have been: 2 officers wounded, 16 men killed, and 83 wounded, a much smaller list than the other battalions in the brigade.

WAR DIARY OF THE FIFTH SEAFORTHS

The Somme Offensive, July 1916

The wild war-pipes were calling,
Our hearts were blithe and free
When we went up the valley
To the death we could not see.
Clear lay the wood before us
In the clear summer weather,
But broken, broken, broken
Are the sons of the heather.
Lieut. E. A. Mackintosh, M.C.

Ten hours after reaching Acq the battalion was on the move again, and by motor lorry, route march, and train, it arrived at Buire in the valley of the Ancre on the morning of 21st July.

By this time the first phase of the Somme offensive was ended. The enemy had been driven from La Boiselle and Fricourt, two of his greatest strongholds, but he still held Thiepval, the strongest of all, so that the British front on our arrival was a great salient running through Contalmaison, in front of Bazentin-le-Grand and Bazentin-le-Petit to the southern edge of High Wood and thence to Delville Wood, and Guillemont. On our arrival, the 153rd and 154th Brigades took over the front along the southern edge of High Wood, and made several desperate but unsuccessful attempts to drive the enemy from this commanding and powerful position.

The general opinion in these brigades was that the strength of the enemy's defences in this rather dense wood was underestimated, that insufficient time was given to the Division to reconnoitre the position, and that the artillery preparation, also through lack of knowledge, did not sufficiently destroy the barbed wire entanglements and machine-gun nests hidden among the trees.

Be the reasons what they may, the attacks, though gallantly persisted in, were a comparative failure, and many valuable lives were lost. Our battalion, on the evening of the 21st, as part of the 152nd Brigade in reserve, marched out of Buire and headed up the valley towards Fricourt. Passing what remained of the village, it swung into a grassy field at the edge of Fricourt Wood and there bivouacked for the night.

Across the valley lay Mametz village and in front of us one could see the dark mass of Mametz Wood, soon to be only too well known to us.

Next morning the enemy aeroplanes must have observed the concentration of troops here, for in the early afternoon the Boche started a bombardment of the valley and road so that for a time things were decidedly warm. Having accepted the task of showing some corps cyclists the route to the headquarters of our other brigades further up, when I got halfway I rather regretted having in a soft moment volunteered my services. We halted on the edge of a ruined village at the top of a rise, from which a splendid view of the whole valley could be got. Further up the valley was a mass of bursting shells (shrapnel and high explosive), the road in particular getting it very heavily. Remembering that our own boys were lying in the open on the opposite side of the valley, where the shells were bursting freely, I felt certain that they must have scores of casualties, so steadily were the shells dropping around them. In a few minutes up the broken, shattered road came limbered waggon after limbered waggon, each drawn by its six horses galloping furiously and tearing the heavy ammunition limbers after them, the drivers hanging on for dear life as the waggons bumped and pitched on the atrocious surface. The poor brutes seemed terror-stricken as they tore past, and no wonder, for below was a perfect inferno. Then came five or six riderless horses, which were caught by some of my party at the top of the rise and handed over to the military police. Then came poor brutes with wounds in their sides and legs.

By and by a lull came, and we pushed on for some hundreds of yards. On going round a curve we came on other evidences of the shelling. Here were two fine grey horses yoked to a limber lying at the side of the road in a pool of blood. Further down lay a horse here and a horse there, while the wounded and dead men had been removed into a field dressing-station, which providentially stood in a recess where

74

some dug-outs had been made for it. Here the stretcher-bearers were very busy bandaging wounded and putting them into the motor ambulances to be taken further back, while a little stream of slightly wounded (arm, head, etc.) was met passing up the road. Further down, we came upon a water waggon split in two by a shell, and here again we had to take shelter as the " strafing " once more increased in intensity.

Finally, we made another rush for our destination, some of the men confessing they had never ridden so hard in their lives, and no sooner were we in the dug-out than the third spasm began, some shells falling just outside and all along the road we had traversed a minute or two before. The return journey was also done in record time, three-quarters of it on the rim in my case, but urgent private affairs prevented repairs until I got back to Divisional head-quarters.

From the 22nd to the 26th the battalion bivouacked in the open, but had twice to change its camping ground owing to severe shelling.

Here we are quite close to Becourt Château where we had such a cheery time a year ago.

While in reserve " Dunvegan," the " Duke " and some others set off one evening to revisit their old dug-outs. They found them still intact, " Faither's " old abode with the carriage door being as it was when they left it. They then visited " Dunvegan Castle " and " Dunrobin," finding them also in good repair, " Dunrobin " having apparently been renovated and improved in the interval. On 27th August 1915, " Dunvegan's " birthday had been celebrated in these dug-outs, and on that occasion " the Duke " had had a bottle of O.P. in " Dunrobin Castle." Next morning " the Duke " was suddenly called away on billeting duties, and, expecting to return, he " planked " (rather a common phrase for a Castle) the O.P. in a gap between a lateral beam of the ducal roof and the roof itself. The battalion never returned there, and the O.P. was wiped off the slate as " lost stores."

When " the Duke " on this occasion revisited his castle, he remembered his loss, and, as a sort of forlorn hope, he inserted his hand into the gap, and lo, and behold! produced the bottle just as he had left it eleven months before. It can readily be appreciated that, in this land of compulsory abstinence, the bottle was not returned to its recess, but taken to " Faither's " dug-out where health to the battalion and confusion to the Boche were heartily drunk, " Dunvegan's " exclamation being, " It must have been English regiments who have occupied this billet since 27th August," his idea being that a Scotch nose would have soon scented out such potent stuff. " The Earl " has been in a semi-morose state ever since owing to the fact that, though invited to join the party, he had refused the invitation.

On the night of the 26th a move was made to Mametz Wood, a reserve position, but one more hated than the front line in High Wood.

Almost continuously the enemy rained all types of shells upon it, there were no dug-outs, not even shelters of any strength, so that there was practically no cover except a few hastily-dug trenches and funk holes, and these afforded poor protection against perfect tornadoes of high explosive and shrapnel, while gas shells also accounted for many, with the result that our five days' occupancy of the wood cost us 130 men.

The 30th was one of those days of terrific enemy fire. Running along the south-western edge of Mametz Wood lies a long valley with a steep bank on its southern side, a valley which has been well and terribly named Death Valley, for the Angel of the Shadow seems continually hovering over it, snapping the golden thread of one here and one there, as he pauses in his flight.

Yet in spite of the perfect inferno of bursting shells, concentrated on this narrow valley and road, the gun limbers went steadily up and down carrying their precious and necessary loads of shells to our guns which were banked almost wheel to wheel on the slope behind Bazentin Wood, and were firing furiously all the afternoon and evening, in another of our attacks on High Wood, an attack which resulted in a small advance of two or three hundred yards into the Wood.

On the 28th Lieut.-Col. Spooner, D.S.O., who has commanded the battalion since January, relinquished his command, having been promoted Brigadier-General of the 183rd Inf. Bde. His smile and cheery " Always merry and bright, boys!" will long be remembered by all who served under him.

The battalion during its spell of duty in the High Wood trenches was under the command of Major Macmillan until Col. Montgomerie of the 1st Norfolks took command on the 7th.

Although there was no actual attack while the battalion was in the High Wood trenches, yet by quiet persistent work the front line trenches were converted from shallow scrapes and disconnected fragments into a deep continuous trench line, well wired in, with good communication trenches leading to the rear, while by steady sapping and connecting up sap heads a new line of trenches was formed 200 yards further into the wood.

During this spell, the battalion had the misfortune to lose Regt.-Sergt.-Major Don Sutherland, D.C.M. and Croix de Guerre, one of the most efficient and most popular Sergt.-Majors any unit could have. He was dangerously wounded while superintending the issue of water in the front line, and, although he ultimately recovered, he did not return to the battalion, much to its regret.

Finally relieved on 7th August, we went into bivouacs at Edgehill.

During 17 days in the Somme offensive, our casualties amounted to 10 officers and 215 other ranks killed and wounded.

ARMENTIÈRES

19th August saw the battalion in billets in Armentières, a large manufacturing town on the borders of Belgium and France, which, though quite close to the front, at that time had suffered comparatively little from shell-fire, owing, it is understood, to a tacit arrangement that, if we left Lille alone, the German gunners would respect Armentières.

In spite of this, it gets shelled spasmodically, and its eastern suburb Houplines is practically in ruins, but in the main part of the town some 6000 French civilians out of a pre-war population of 30,000 still went about their usual occupations, and shops, *estaminets*, and even laundries carried on as usual.

Here again as at Festubert, the ground is water-logged and trenches have to be built up with sand-bags.

The stay here was a quiet and uneventful one and on 19th September the battalion was relieved and went into camp close to Bailleul, where it remained for rest and training until the 30th when it entrained for Doullens, and after billeting for a few days at Gezancourt went into the trenches in front of Hebuterne on 4th October.

Here until the 16th work went on practically without ceasing, new communication trenches being dug, bomb stores built, telephone cables buried, forward gun positions dug and camouflaged, shells stacked beside them, and heavy trench mortars placed in position, all pointing to an imminent attack on the strong German position of Hebuterne ; and then suddenly came orders cancelling all further preparations for the attack, and withdrawing the Division from the line. Rumour had it that a too loquacious artillery observation officer in a forward post had given the prospective attack, even as to objective and date, away, through indiscreet chatter with a friend over the phone, and that this had been picked up by a German listening set, although how the British high command found out about the leakage is another matter.

These listening sets, both Allied and German, are most useful. They are somewhat similar to a wireless set, and can pick up conversations and Morse code messages at a distance of one or two miles from the phone lines through which the message is passing, owing to leakage of current from insufficiently insulated cable.

These leakages travel as earth waves, and are picked up and so magnified by the set's delicate receivers, that the conversations are sometimes more distinctly heard by the operator at the listening set than by the people actually conversing together.

That artillery officer was certainly the most heartily anathematized man in the Division as the one who had rendered all our hard work in mud and rain, and our cold and dreary bivouacking on the wind-swept plain at Courcelles in the biting October winds of no avail.

BEAUMONT-HAMEL, 13TH NOVEMBER 1916

In the cold of the morning
A grey mist was drawn
Over the waves
That went up in the dawn,
Went up like the waves
Of the wild Northern Sea;
For the North has arisen,
The North has broke free.

Ghosts of the heroes
That died in the Wood
Looked on the killing
And saw it was good.
Far over the hillsides
They saw in their dream
The kilted men charging,
The bayonets gleam.

LIEUT. E. A. MACKINTOSH.

On 17th October the battalion moved some miles further south to Mailly-Maillet, the Division taking over the front facing Beaumont-Hamel, a ruined village, a mile north of the Ancre, which the Germans had by two years' steady work converted into a most formidable stronghold rivalling Thiepval on the south of the river.

The village and the trenches in front stood high, and on the southern side it was flanked by the " Y " ravine with steep banks in which were numerous deep dug-outs where thousands of men could safely withstand the heaviest bombardment.

In front of the village were at least three main trench systems well connected up, with deep dug-outs, and the barbed wire entanglements, machine-gun posts and trench-mortar emplacements were constructed with that attention to detail and that desire for security for which the Boche is famous.

The village itself, by means of reinforced concrete backings to its ruined walls, forming powerful machine-gun posts, by subterranean passages between its cellars and caves, and by trenches dug in its streets, formed a further system even more difficult to master than the powerful trenches in front.

From 17th October the work was a repetition of the work in front of Hebuterne, and the weather, as usual with almost any British advance, seemed to favour those children of the devil, the Boche, for it rained persistently, converting camps (and the majority of the battalion were under canvas) into quagmires, and trenches into impossible sloughs, the soft clay continually falling in and blocking up even the best revetted, and yet bombs, artillery ammunition, and the thousand and one requisites of an attack were in position some days before the attack took place.

At last two fine days came, and on the night of the 12th-13th the attacking infantry went up into the line.

For several days, our guns had been battering away at irregular intervals at the enemy's wire and trenches, while our heavier artillery devoted their attention to the areas behind, shelling his reserves, his dumps, his railways stations and depots.

Tanks were also in readiness, although the general consensus of opinion was that, from the terrible nature of the country, it would be impossible for them to make much headway, and so it proved, for only one got as far as the enemy front line and sat astride it, unable to go backward or forward.

The morning was dark and misty, and long before Zero hour the first waves had climbed out of the knee-deep trenches and lay upon the parapet.

At 5.45 a.m. the signal, the exploding of a mine, was given, our artillery opened a terrific barrage fire on the German front line, and over went the infantry, not doubling, not even walking, but wading knee-deep and sometimes waist-deep through the morass of sticky mud and water and neck-deep shell-holes which constituted no-man's land.

The 5th Seaforths had the honour of leading the attack on one sector of the village, with their left flank on the Auchonvillers-Beaumont-Hamel road, their final objective being a German trench line 200 yards east of the village. The enemy's machine-gun fire and uncut wire in the centre held up the advance for a time so that the barrage went too far ahead, while, owing to the dense fog, direction was lost, and the attack split up into small parties, yet, in spite of these difficulties, the first German line was easily carried, except for one or two isolated points where the enemy put up a good fight.

Dropping into the trench, sentries were posted at the dug-out doors, while a few bombs were sent down as a gentle reminder of our presence.

The first wave held this trench, and arranged for disposal of prisoners, etc., while the second, third, and fourth waves passed on to the succeeding trenches. The second line was also soon captured, but for the third line the fighting was more stubborn, a machine-gun post and some snipers effectually sweeping the ground of our advance.

Two bombing parties were hurriedly formed who advanced along the trenches, killed the machine gunners and captured their guns.

To get these and the snipers a party had to enter and pass through a dug-out, and climb a stair into a concrete apertured little fort, the holders of which were thoroughly surprised at their secret entrance having been discovered.

In the evening the battalion, which by that time consisted of 90 men under Major Robertson with Capts. Morrison and Murray and Lieuts. Lupton and Mackay, went through Beaumont-Hamel, and consolidated the final objective as arranged.

By 4 p.m. the Division had gained its objective, and the complete defensive system was in our hands, while over 1700 prisoners, of whom the 5th Seaforths claimed 600, had been sent to the rear.

Some of the rather humorous incidents of the battle are worth relating.

One big dug-out of Boches was being slowly emptied of its occupants by a party of our men. As each Boche appeared at the dug-out entrance with the ever-ready " Merci, Kamerad ! " on his lips, our fellows, plastered with mud from head to foot, and soaked to the skin, were so annoyed at their spick-and-span appearance, that each man, as he rather hesitatingly emerged, got a kick to help him on his way down the trench, not a fierce, vindictive kick with sting in it, but one of a genial cheerio type.

The " Duke " carried a bottle of whisky in his left greatcoat pocket for use in case of wounds or fatigue. Just before Zero hour, he pulled the cork, and lightly replaced it, so as to be ready for emergencies. When half-way across no-man's land, he suddenly thought of what would happen if a machine-gun bullet took his precious bottle, and, thereafter, he advanced with his right shoulder forward, so as to afford some protection for it. The bottle got safely into Beaumont-Hamel and was left there.

In connection with this fight, the 51st Division has a grudge against the Naval Division, which was on its right, and especially with a man of peace in that Division, who for the nonce had seemingly become a man of war.

One battalion officer, dressed for attack in private's kilt and tunic, was, with a small party, marshalling 600 prisoners for leading to the rear, when this padre, with a stronger party, rushed up and demanded that the prisoners should be handed over to him.

On the officer demurring, the padre, so the story goes, knocked him into a shell-hole, and took the prisoners to the Naval Division.

On a protest being lodged, the Naval Division offered to go halves, but, as we could afford to be generous, they were told to keep them.

The battalion remained in the line until the night of the 14th–15th, and during that time repelled numerous attacks.

During these two days the casualties were: 94 killed or died of wounds, 193 wounded and 5 missing, among these being 2 officers, Lieuts. A. Mackay and B. Holroyd killed, and 9 wounded.

THE 1916 CAMPAIGN

Major Robertson, as senior officer in the advance, displayed great coolness, working out the proper line of advance by compass when sense of direction was lost owing to the fog. He collected the scattered parties under heavy fire and when attacked by an enemy bombing party he drove them off, and finally led his men to the fourth line which he consolidated and held.

2nd Lieut. A. J. Mackay, when held up at the second line, put his men in a defensive position and with two men went out to reconnoitre. He took a party of 60 men by surprise and made them prisoners.

On reaching the third line, his party was completely cut off, but he held on until reinforcements came up.

2nd Lieut. F. Lupton organized bombing parties, and when some one gave the order to retire, and the men hesitated, he countermanded the order, rallied the men and pushed on.

By the night of the 19th the battalion was once again in the line, being required to strengthen the defences against the enemy's furious counter-attacks, for well he knew that, Beaumont-Hamel lost, it was only a matter of time for a general withdrawal of his line. There they remained until the night of the 24th, their last effort being a heroic but futile attempt to relieve 80 men of another Division who had been cut off some days previously, and who had managed to send back word that they were still holding out.

In this battle the battalion earned high praise for its fighting qualities, one staff officer saying, " The 5th were simply ' It,' doing all and more than all they were asked to do, in much less time than even the most optimistic staff officer thought possible."

The Corps Commander, writing to the Division after the battle said, " All the world looks upon the capture of Beaumont-Hamel as one of the greatest feats of the war, and to those who know the ground and defences it must always be a marvellously fine performance."

Among the honours awarded were the D.S.O. to Major J. J. Robertson and M.C.'s to 2nd Lieuts. Lupton and A. J. Mackay, with a M.M. bar to Coy.-Sergt.-Major Goddard and 10 M.M.'s.

THE COURCELETTE SECTOR, DECEMBER 1916

On relief, the battalion went back to Forceville, where strong drafts brought it up to strength, and on the 28th it moved to Bouzincourt, just behind Albert.

Here five restful days were spent in training the new men in battalion methods of attack, but on the 4th December a move forward was made to the Bruce hut behind Aveluy, for once again the Division was in the line.

In the autumn the Germans had been driven still

further back towards Bapaume, and to the 51st was assigned the task of manning that section of the line which lay in front of Courcelette, a village slightly north of the Albert-Bapaume main road, a task which in some respects was the "rottenest" the Division had to do in France.

This area, water-logged by several months' persistent rain, pitted with the innumerable shell-holes of the Somme offensive, with every town and village reduced to heaps of brick and chalk, and precious little even of these, with no deep dug-outs, no proper trench system, and no communication trenches, such an area in the depth of winter was a veritable death-trap so far as sickness and trench feet were concerned, and in it battalions simply faded away day by day.

Of all the desolation of desolations ever pictured by man this is the worst.

We read of countries in olden times being laid waste by fire and sword, but fire and sword must have caused a small, a trivial desolation, compared to that wrought by the thousands upon thousands of high explosive shells rained upon this sad countryside for days and weeks on end. Then add to this, the scientifically destructive efforts of the Hun on retiring, in blowing up cross-roads, and exploding mines in the cellars of every house still bearing the semblance of a house, in cutting down every tree, and, in fact, every fruit-bearing bush, in bleaching and burning all vegetation by his poison gas, and you can perhaps form a faint picture of the ghastliness of this once fair district.

Here we first enjoyed the comparative comfort of Nissen Huts, for in this area there were several camps of them, and what a boon they were to the men after spending several months wearily in tents and bivouacs. Oblong in plan and semicircular in elevation, with a wooden floor raised a foot or more above the ground, with sides of curved corrugated iron, lined inside with match boarding and supplied with a Canadian sheet-iron stove which can burn practically anything but bully beef tins, they give troops coming out of the line some chance to dry and clean themselves, and live in comparative comfort while in reserve, even if thirty men and even more are crowded into one hut.

Quickly erected and easily taken to pieces, the pioneers can in a day or two shift a camp to suit the needs of the situation, and it is safe to say that thousands of lives have been saved by their use in the last two winter campaigns of the war.

As we go up the great Albert-Bapaume road to our front line at Courcelette, we have some opportunity of studying the effects of modern war.

Passing through Albert, which had not yet suffered its final martyrdom—that took place in March 1918— and over which the Virgin and Child still looked piti-fully down, we breast the rise with grassy fields on either side, and then dip into the old British and

German front line trenches at La Boiselle, with the old rusty barbed wire still lying as artillery fire left it in July.

La Boiselle itself is simply a series of mounds and craters. Not a fragment of a house remains. The village churchyard and church stood at the angle of the cross-roads, but one could pass it many times without recognizing it unless he chanced to observe among the chalk mounds a fragment or two of polished stone or a spike or two of iron cross. As one cynic remarked, " I'm afraid there'll be some quarrels about the family lairs and vaults when the inhabitants return."

Further on, we saw on the left-hand side of the valley the remains of Ovillers, but the only semblance of buildings we could see was a jagged bit of brick-work about 10 feet high and 2 or 3 feet thick, with a notice-board : " Ovillers Church. Do not touch."

A mile or more further on we came to what was once Pozieres, a town of 2000 inhabitants, which had been captured after a terrible struggle by the Australians on 25th July.

Now it consisted of small mounds of brick and chalk, with lines of tree stumps 2 or 3 feet high, marking where once the side streets and orchards had been, but as to houses or fragments of houses, there were none, the only thing above ground level being the remains, on the left-hand side of the road, of a German reinforced concrete obstruction post, and it even was but a fragment.

The ground is pitted and honeycombed with shell craters; derelict aeroplanes, their torn canvas fluttering dismally, lie around, and one or two derelict tanks still lie where the conqueror, mud, or a direct hit forced them to remain.

This village is now full of our guns, placed, in many instances, side by side in sunken roads, great 8, 9'2, and 12-inch guns, each with its little store of those fat weighty important-looking shells which every now and then they send smashing into the enemy's lines or rest billets behind.

Further up, past the famous wind-mill, we come into the area of 18-pounders, then to the infantry in support doing their best to construct dug-outs and shelters in sunken roads to shield them a little from the cold, and finally we arrive, but not by day, at the British front line.

Here a winding track of duckboards has been laid twisting and twining among the innumerable shell-holes which lie almost lip to lip, and woe betide the one who in the darkness misses the track, for he is almost certain to go head first into a shell-hole full of icy water, in which at least two of our men were drowned.

One very dignified General was coming out one dark night with two of his officers, when he disappeared with a mighty splash, and his subordinates had to pull him out of a 6-foot shell-hole, a dripping spectacle of mud and water. His startled thoughts were too profound for words, so he took it in silence.

All movement by day in this area was forbidden, the slightest movement brought machine-gun fire and even sniping with whizz-bangs, with the result that the men sat from 7 a.m. to 5 p.m. up to the knees or waists in mud and water, with no hot food, until they were utterly benumbed, and had lost all sense of feeling in their feet and legs.

As a consequence many men collapsed and on relief had to be carried out on the backs of their sturdier neighbours. Our battalion had three spells of duty in this torture chamber, and lost over 100 men with trench feet during that time, while the most wretched New Year's Day that any one could wish to spend was spent here by two companies of the battalion.

One night a big Prussian Guardsman, carrying a pannikin of hot coffee, came walking into our lines. He had gone back for his issue of coffee to his second line, and, returning, had passed between two sections of his own front trench and unsuspectingly walked into ours.

Our artillery observation officer, going up to his forward station, entered what he thought was our front line. Finding no one, he crawled along until he found some equipment which he knew to be Boche, so he quietly crept back in the direction he had come. As he could not find his post he elected to squat in a shell-hole until the first peep of daylight; and, when this came, to his disgust he found he had shivered all night within 50 yards of his slightly more comfortable post.

The command of the battalion was taken over by Lieut.-Col. Wm. Macfarlane, D.S.O., of the 15th H.L.I. on 12th January and on the 13th we bade farewell to the Courcelette sector, and, after a three days' march, went into rest billets at Le Titre, where we remained until 5th February.

CHAPTER IV

THE 1917 CAMPAIGN

THE ARRAS OFFENSIVE, APRIL 1917

ON 5th February the battalion was once more on the move along frosty, ice-bound roads, and on the 10th arrived at Ecoivres behind our old Labyrinth sector of last spring.

Here once again the old round of preparation for an attack was begun, and continued without intermission until the battle of Arras on 9th April.

The Divisional front here is based on the villages of Ecurie and Roclincourt, the former standing high in the triangle between the Arras-Souchez and Arras-Lens roads, the latter lying a little nearer the line but in the valley. Our trenches lie in this low-lying flat country, but in front we can see the famous Vimy Ridge, and behind it we know lies the busy town of Lens.

On 19th February the battalion had to mourn the loss of Lieut.-Col. Macfarlane, D.S.O., who had only held the command for six weeks, when he was got by an enemy sniper when going round the front line and instantaneously killed. He was buried with full military honours in the little soldiers' cemetery at Maroeuil, a cemetery consisting largely of the gallant dead of the 51st Division.

The command was then taken over by Col. J. M. Scott of the 9th Argyll and Sutherland Highlanders.

Since coming to this sector we have been very busy. The weather has been simply diabolical, scarcely a day without rain and cold biting winds. (Puir auld Scotland, shall we ever again complain of your variable climate ?) The natives tell us that this spot has been a paradise since we left it on 11th July 1916, but I made the prophecy that our Division's arrival meant a stirring up of the locality ; and in truth it has been so, and no mistake.

During the first ten days we had a fine time, as the frost still held and the trenches and roads were hard bound and firm. A haze hung over the country, scarcely a shot, either rifle or gun, was fired. We could walk across the open almost to the front line, and every one said that this was a " bon " spot.

Then the conditions changed. The frost vanished, the haze disappeared, the trenches became quagmires of mud and water, the roads became oceans of mud and the motor lorries scooped out the whole foundations of the softened roads, leaving holes 2 or 3 feet deep for the next waggon or lorry to plough through. Then the soft-hearted Saxons who confronted us were withdrawn and their places were again taken by those dour, dogged Bavarians, who faced us a year ago. Artillery, rifle, machine-gun and trench-mortar fire gradually became intensified as the days went on, until our overland walks had to be entirely suspended and we were forced to keep to the trenches.

And such trenches they were after the frost—sticky, gluey mud, in which if you stood for thirty seconds you stuck fast and had to grab something while you tried to pull out one leg, which, whenever you took the next step, sunk as deeply as before, and necessitated the same process, step by step, so that in bad bits one took an hour to go 200 yards. Some men came back in their socks, their boots, if a biggish size, being left in the mud.

Our own battalion had several spells of this life, both in the front line and supports, and as we were working double time preparing for the spring and the termination of the war, as we thought, the work was very hard, and my heart was often sore for the poor boys toiling through it. When even I, with nothing but my own weight to carry, stuck fast, imagine the physical strain on a private carrying on his shoulder a box of Stokes gun bombs, a box of rifle ammunition, a heavy bag of rations, two petrol tins of water, or any of the other and numerous things the fatigue man has to carry plus his rifle and 150 rounds of ammunition, and you will have some idea of

what the private has to endure. Further, he may go
for a week or more without being able to get his boots
dried, he may have to put on the same semi-dry socks
in the morning that he puts off at night, and he may
get soaked through to the skin and have no chance of
changing or drying his clothes except by wearing them
and letting the heat of the body do so. And yet how
wonderfully cheery our boys are, smiling in the face
of all these hardships, plus the chance of sudden death
from the multifold death-dealing devices of modern
warfare.

I heard two good stories the other day.

A certain General, noted for his courtesy, was passing
up the trenches and met two men carrying a stretcher
with a man completely wrapped up in a brown blanket,
the usual sign that the burden is one who has been
killed.

Stepping to one side to let them pass, the General
stood at attention, saluted, and said, " Your General
salutes you, gallant dead."

An erratic arm swept the blanket to one side, and an
unsteady voice said, " What's the auld fool saying
noo ? "

The burden was not by any means dead, but was a
weaker vessel who had been entrusted with the carrying
up of his Company's rum, of which he had imbibed
such a quantity that he became utterly helpless, and
two friends in need, to save him from further trouble,

had put him on a stretcher and were carrying him away to a quieter spot. History does not record what the General said, or what the fate of the burden was.

A labour battalion for work on roads lay beside us here and at 9 a.m. one day there was a sick parade under a sergeant. Twenty-five men paraded, and the sergeant formed them up in two ranks, 12 in front and 13 behind, numbered them and then gave the command, " Form fours right." This being done, he found that he had an odd man, whom he, being pretty much a novice in matters of drill, could not assimilate into the decorous evenness of fours. After trying to work No. 25 in several times, he gave it up in despair, and said, " Look here, you, fall out ; you won't parade before the doctor to-day." And sick or not sick, No. 25 had to fall out and wait for a future medical parade.

Early in March, conditions became harder; the Boche realizing that an offensive was coming here, brought up more guns, mortars, aeroplanes and infantry with the result that things began to hum, and trenches were smashed right and left. Fighting between our own and enemy aeroplanes became more and more active, and the British mastery of the air so glibly talked about at home at this time was in no sense manifest here, the Boche having undoubtedly the faster and better machines. To see, day after day, our slow buses, unprotected by fast scouts, being swooped down upon from the higher levels by a fast German machine, to see our fellows trying to escape by twisting and diving, like a heron from an eagle, while the Boche makes circles round them, pouring in belts of ammunition, and then to see our plane turning over and over, or, worse still, to see it come down a mass of flames, made one gnash his teeth, and wish that some of those " stay at home " aeroplane experts were placed on some of these slow products of theirs, and sent over the enemy line, instead of the brave lads who, when they ascend, know they are going to almost certain death.

All preparations having been completed, at 5 a.m. on 9th April all the artillery on this front opened a terrific fire, and then over went our infantry. It was a bitterly cold morning with a strong wind and heavy rain showers, changing into snow later on. Line after line of enemy trenches was taken, although the Bavarians on our front, the finest fighting material in the German army, fought stubbornly, some groups holding out until every man was killed.

Machine guns, as in Beaumont-Hamel, did most mischief, but snipers also accounted for many. Our own men, along with the 6th Seaforth Highlanders, formed the attacking waves of the left half of the 152nd Brigade's front, to the 6th being allotted the first system of enemy trenches while the 5th had to take the second and third systems.

THE 1917 CAMPAIGN

Early in the attack, our first waves were held up by the fire of two enemy machine guns, seeing which Sergts. Elder and J. Ross worked up a light railway under the shelter of a bank, and scuppered the machine gunners, thus allowing the advance to proceed, and also providing a position from which a Lewis gun enfiladed the German trench, killing many of the enemy, and enabling the party to work along the trench, capturing two more machine guns and a battalion headquarters.

After determined fighting all day, the second enemy system was taken by our men at 2.15 p.m., and the third and final objective at 3.15 p.m. Here " B " Company captured seven German officers, including one of high rank, and a number of men. Of the 16 officers who went over the top in this battle, one, Lieut. Moore, was killed and nine wounded, while 59 other ranks were killed, 229 wounded, and 10 posted as missing.

I visited the field of battle the day after and what sad sights I saw! Surely after the carnage and misery among the nations of the world by this wholesale slaughter, nations will agree that war is to cease and that peace is to reign hereafter !

Here were our own men, one here, another there, each lying as he had fallen from bullet or shell, his rifle still in his hand. Here were men carrying in the dead and collecting them in one place, while others were digging a huge grave in which the men are now buried side by side. One grave of this sort I saw being dug in no-man's land between where our own and the enemy front lines were until the day before.

In one little corner of a trench lay about twenty dead Boches, fine stalwart men, who, one private told me, had put up a good fight. While our troops advanced some of these men worked their machine gun while the others hurled bombs as they came nearer, and actually fought on until the last man was killed.

One party of Boches started throwing bombs at an officer and man of ours lying wounded near their trench, and so incensed were our men that none of these went back prisoners ; can one wonder at it ?

On 11th April the battalion was relieved and went into rest billets at X and Y huts on the Arras-St. Pol road, but on the 17th a move was made to Arras where the men were billeted in empty houses, and on the 19th they were once more in the line near Fampoux on the river Scarpe, a sector slightly south of our last.

The enemy had, on the 9th, been driven from the vicinity of Arras, several miles up the river, and here his front was slightly beyond Fampoux, once a pleasant village on the canalised Scarpe, but now deserted and badly smashed.

THE 1917 CAMPAIGN

THE SCARPE, 23RD APRIL 1917

On 23rd April began one of the most stubbornly contested battles of the war, and once again our Division was in the thick of it. East of Fampoux and close to the river stands the village of Roeux and just north of it astride the railway running up the Scarpe valley are the now famous Chemical Works, a cluster of factories, dwelling-houses, and railway sidings, which had to be captured at all costs. Two Divisions had already tried and failed to take the objective set before us, but with a mighty effort our men managed to attain what was regarded as the impossible, and that in spite of tremendous enemy efforts.

For several days the battle swayed to and fro, our men gaining a point, then the Boche counter-attacking with thousands of fresh troops and driving us out, then our men pressing forward once again, until at last we gained and consolidated not what we had aimed at, but a goodly part of it. The artillery fire on both sides was the heaviest on record, the Boche seemingly gathering together as many guns as he could spare from other sectors. His battalions could be seen by our observers being hurried up from the rear along the roads, with the result that we were able to turn our heavies on them while still in close order formation. Some of his battalions were in this way wiped out before they came anywhere near the fighting area. Our casualties in such a fight were necessarily heavy, but once again the percentage of killed and wounded was not excessive.

Providentially for our battalion it was its turn to be in support, and, although it held the line before the opening day and was far up afterwards, it escaped with very few casualties, only four or five being killed and about a dozen wounded.

In the " push " on 9th April Signal work was very much simpler than on this occasion, as we had then a great buried system—50 or 60 pairs of wires buried in trenches from 6 to 8 feet deep, so that it would require a very heavy shell having a direct hit on the " bury " to break the wires. This " bury " had been made previously and from it we ran smaller " buries " of 12 pairs to each Brigade headquarters in the line. These stood the test of the enemy's shelling so that the Brigades were in continuous communication with the Division and artillery all the time. From the brigades there were lines buried 2 or 3 feet deep in the ordinary trenches, but many of these were broken, and lines at the last moment were run out across the open country to each battalion, lines which were maintained by the bravery of the linesmen, who went out under heavy shell-fire and repaired them.

As the companies of each battalion went forward

two or three signallers with a half-mile drum of thin cable went with the second wave, laying out their lines across the country into the German trenches from our own, repairing breaks as they occurred, or sometimes relaying long stretches where the intense shelling had smashed the line to pieces.

In the 23rd April "show" things were very different. We were in what a week or so before had been German territory, and we could not find or utilize very much of his buried system and so we had to depend everywhere on lines laid across the open or hung on the trees. Further, the enemy shelling was much severer than on the 9th, causing much more breaking of the lines.

Beyond the great embankment and about a mile further east stood the ruined village of Athies, and a mile further on stood Fampoux, quite close behind our front line. These two villages got it hard and heavy by the Boche artillery every day and almost every hour of the day. Going up to reconnoitre, we were delighted to see manifest signs of the haste with which the Boche had cleared out.

Here were two great 8-inch guns in their gun pits, with piles of ammunition by them. Further along was a whole battery of 5·9-inch guns and close at hand several batteries of smaller calibre, most of them still facing our old lines. Some enthusiastic heavy trench-mortar people had, however, turned one

of the 8-inch guns round and were steadily battering the enemy with his own shells. This went on all
day until one of the amateur gunners, through leaving a
screw loose, caused the gun itself, when fired, to run
back out of the socket in which it is fixed, until it
lay on the trail; so that ended their little amuse-
ment for the day.

In Fampoux we fixed a signal exchange with lines
coming forward from the Division and radiating right
and left to the two Brigades who were to fight.

We found out that with the ordinary lines we had
laid across country and along the banks of the Scarpe
it would be impossible to maintain communication,
so it was resolved to sink them in the bed of the
river. At 4 a.m. one day a party of four set off to
the river with some coils of armoured cable, a punt
having been secured the night before, and two oars
having been surreptitiously removed from a pontoon
and converted into paddles with the help of the beef
saw of a friendly company cook. Off we pushed on
our little jaunt, two paddling and two paying out the
cables astern. The crew were a little inexperienced
at first, one insisting on back-watering when he was
wanted to keep her head down stream by paddling
vigorously, but with a few tersely uttered hints as to
procedure the ship began to forge ahead and the
cable to get less. Soon we came to Athies (we had
sundry valid and convincing reasons for not dilly-

dallying, as one can't very well take cover from shell-fire in a punt). Here we had a party waiting, with whose help we pulled the boat across the road, and launched her by means of a slope formed by a convenient shell-hole into lower waters beyond. Taking on more cable, we had in two mornings laid four pairs all the way to Fampoux (two miles) with test points every 440 yards on the banks so that a break could be easily localized.

The weather was lovely, the river was beautiful, with rows of stately trees alongside, but the amenities were not of the best, as shells often went splashing into the river itself, sending up fountains of water 50 feet high. So when the last coil was laid the party heaved a sigh of relief at being on terra firma once again, where even a tree trunk gives some protection.

From the ends of these river cables short lines were laid into the cellar of what had once been a rather nice château which had been occupied by the enemy for the past two years and a good time he must have had in it. He had grown acres of cabbages and other vegetables in the garden and the fields around. Some artist had painted rather good pictures on the wall-paper of the principal room, including the usual bombastic one of the typical bullet-headed German soldier with rifle in left hand, and right, with fist clenched, raised aloft, defying all and sundry. Here a party of twelve settled down for the great attack—four runners, for fear of all lines going down, four linesmen, for repairing, and four men for the exchange and other duties. We found the cellar with eight inches of water in it, but with empty petrol tins for cross beams and a Boche partition of planking which we tore down in the rooms above, as a floor, we made a good platform above the water. On the platform we spread our beds when we got a chance to sleep. An old stove in one corner kept the place warm, although terrifically smoky, but most of the cooking was done upstairs, except when the shells came too near. The Boche gave us plenty of fire-wood, for in the last four or five days of our residence he completely altered the house above, knocking one gable completely in, lifting off part of the roof and generally supplying smashed doors, windows and wooden shutters, which were of no use except as firewood.

The cellar stood all right, and although the river lines were broken three or four times yet the faithful punt was soon on the scene and the fault was localized and repaired by hauling in the cable until you came to the break, so that at least two pairs out of the four were always through, and that sufficed.

To the brigades which lay right and left of the cellar, one 500 yards away and the other 900, four lines each were laid as widely apart as possible, and yet so terrific was the enemy shelling the night before the attack that a line 1500 yards long, laid at 11 a.m., took two linesmen from 9 p.m. to 2 a.m. to go along it, mending at least 50 breaks and at last giving it up in disgust until daylight, as at some cuts, although they crawled about on their hands and knees and even used a torch to find the forward part of the break, they couldn't, so far had the explosion thrown the cut line. However, the other three pairs were kept through by strenuous efforts, and that was good enough.

At 4.15 a.m. on 23rd April, after a rather quiet morning, our guns all started to pump shells into the German lines and in a second or two the din was terrific. I climbed to a ruined attic and looked forward but nothing could be seen but a wall of smoke caused by the bursting shells. The Boche soon replied, and considering the cellar a healthier spot than an attic I retired there.

After an hour or so of this over went our infantry towards the German lines. They were met by artillery and machine-gun fire, but pushed on, into and through the enemy's first trenches, capturing a number of prisoners. As the early morning light improved, the battle raged all the fiercer and the steady tap, tap, tap of the machine guns increased in density. Several " tanks " went forward in the attack.

The Chemical Works was found to be a German fortress of cellars, dug-outs and machine-gun emplacements, but our men swarmed through it and quickly had it in their hands. Then came a tremen-

dous counter-attack of infantry, strongly supported by
heavy artillery fire, and our men were forced to withdraw. Rallied, they came on again and drove the
Boche out, with the result that the position has now
been pounded so much by the heavy artillery of both
sides that it is untenable by either, and lies between
the British and German fronts.

What made the shooting of the Boche more deadly
was the fact that he knew exactly where every trench,
village, building and bridge was, with the result that
he could get the exact range with his guns, and yet
the escapes were marvellous. The upper end of the
trenches where our battalion lay for several days was
in full view of the enemy. Most of the men slept
under canvas sheets from the lack of dug-outs, and
yet the casualties of the battalion were marvellously
slight.

A little description of what a Signaller has to come
through will give one a faint idea of the still greater
risks and dangers run by our gallant infantry. After
twenty-six hours' steady work laying and repairing
lines, two of them decided to leave their watery cellar
and make their way back along the river bank to the
embankment.

Leaving about 2.30 a.m., they doubled out at the
back door through a gap in the wall and across the
fields to the river. At this time the Boche was shelling
the two villages, but they were between the two

barrages and were fairly safe. By and by they came
to a big wooden bridge across the river (erected by
the Boche) and crossed this to the tow-path at the
other side. Here they smelt gas, and could hear the
peculiar whine of the gas shells and the slight " phut "
they gave as they burst. They put on their gas masks
and sat tight to see if there would come a lull as they
could see and hear both types of shells bursting in the
next village and along the tow-path. Getting tired
of waiting, they scrambled on again. It is very
difficult to see at night with a gas helmet on, and
they had the danger of falling into the river or tumbling
into a shell-hole plus their other troubles. They had
got about thirty trees down the bank when a gas shell
burst against the tree in front, so they crouched behind
another tree and waited. Then followed a perfect
tornado of these shells, right and left and in front,
so they lay as flat as the proverbial flounder behind
their trees and waited. When shells fell into the river
and burst they made a hissing sound like a mammoth
Seidlitz powder and then came a mighty splutter, and
lumps of frothy water were thrown all over them at
times.

At last they came to the conclusion they could not
go forward, so they decided to dodge back from tree
to tree to the bridge as giving head cover. They had
several tumbles, as the night was dark, and one got
the shock of his life when he went head first into a big

shell-hole with 4 or 5 feet of water and mud in it. However, personal appearance does not count at times such as these, so they ultimately reached the bridge and gasped for breath for some time, as a gas mask isn't exactly the best oxygen supplying apparatus for a sprint. Having debated the matter as to going back to where they had started from or striking up to the public road, they decided for the latter. Across the bridge they went, there meeting two of the battalion signallers, both in gas masks, looking for some hypothetical lines they were to pick up. Right across country they went, stumbling and floundering, until one thought of turning down his glass goggles and gripping the part that presses on the nose with one hand to keep it on. Then taking his companion by the hand, as he had the older type and couldn't do this, they made better speed in avoiding shell-holes. Getting to the top of the rise near the road they ran into another type of annoyance, for the Boche started shelling this point with big black crumps. One arrived simultaneously with them, and quite close, so they bolted for an old trench which they could dimly make out. They got cover and tried to feel as small as possible, while old " Fritz " pounded away for at least half an hour. A lull coming, one crawled forth to look for his companion, but his hopes of a lull were rather premature, for once again the shelling started, but both found dug-outs.

Here they waited until morning dawned, when they set off, getting to bed at 6 a.m. With three hours' sleep they were up again and worked without a break for thirty-six hours, when tired nature asserted itself and both slept for ten hours, never moving although the château had two direct hits in the time.

On 26th April the battalion, on relief, went into rest billets at Mont-en-Ternois, where it remained until 10th May enjoying a spell of beautiful weather which did much to improve the condition of the men.

THE CHEMICAL WORKS, ROEUX, MAY 1917

On 11th May, however, we were back in the same battle area, east of Fampoux.

Here our front line was to the west of Roeux cemetery, the Division which had succeeded ours having in the interval lost the greater part of the village.

One of the first things the battalion did on taking over, was to push forward on the night of the 13th and occupy the eastern end of Roeux, at the same time establishing posts on the Roeux-Plouvain road. We retook this area with scarcely any casualties, although the Boche snipers, hidden in the houses, caused some trouble, until our men, entering the houses on the opposite side of the street, replied by counter-sniping, and by this means, and rifle grenades, they soon wiped them out.

For a day peace reigned supreme, and every one began to wonder what the Boche was doing, especially as some prisoners had said that he was to retire to his next line. Then suddenly the enemy's guns opened out, not only his batteries on our front, but also his guns on right and left, directing a converging fire on our narrow front (approximately three-quarters of a mile), for he seemed to have a great desire to get back what he had lost.

Here our men had to endure fifteen hours of the most terrible artillery fire they have yet had. The Somme was nothing to it, and as our front lines were mostly shell-holes and shallow trenches, with few dug-outs, it was a terrible experience.

Towards early morning his fire became heavier and heavier, until it reached its maximum, when he was giving us as heavy a shelling as we have ever given him. Immediately afterwards he advanced with tens of thousands of fresh troops brought up from the rear, and those were hurled at our front. The Chemical Works again became the centre of the storm, and with such fury did he attack that the right battalion of the Division on our left was hurled back, and our men had for a time Boche in front, on their left flank, and behind them.

Our men were fighting stubbornly against tremendous odds, and yet they resisted all his attempts at taking their line. Colonels, Majors, and even tunnellers were fighting for all they were worth, one Colonel accounting for several Boches with a rifle he picked up. Reports came filtering back by wounded, that we had lost the position—a rumour which proved to be untrue, but caused some anxiety, as all our telephone lines forward had been smashed to pieces by the intense fire, and no reliable information was available for some time.

Battalions in support and reserve were hurriedly moved forward, and one of these, coming up at the double with fixed bayonets, charged the Boche and hurled him back in confusion. He could no more stand against our cold steel than a sparrow can stand against a hawk, and he was soon back in his own lines broken and disorganized.

In this battle 2nd Lieut. A. J. Mackay who won the M.C. at Beaumont-Hamel was awarded a bar; for, when cut off in Roeux, he organized defensive posts, and held his position, inflicting heavy losses on the advancing enemy. He then led a counter-attack and drove them back.

2nd Lieut. Donald Simpson, for his bravery in the same fight, won the M.C. Although severely wounded in the morning, he refused to leave his men and go to the dressing-station, and continued doing splendid work all day.

Sergts. A. Morrison, James Mowat, and J. Shaw Kelly also won D.C.M.'s for the exceptionally gallant work they did in helping to save what was an extremely critical situation.

Our men say that it was the finest chance that they have had in this war of meeting the enemy face to face, and I think those Huns who survived will remember it ruefully for the rest of their lives. For once also we had a chance of using rifle fire as it should be used, as he came over in rather close formation, and thousands upon thousands were mowed down, as a scythe mows down a hayfield, by our machine guns and rapid rifle fire.

Congratulatory wires were afterwards received from the Army and Corps Commanders.

The Army Commander's wire said, " Convey to 51st Division my congratulations on their gallantry at Roeux and Chemical Works on 16th May," while the Corps Commander wired, " Heartiest congratulations to you all on fine work of 15th and 16th, and especially to General Pelham Burn and 152nd Inf. Bde. whose tenacity and pluck saved an awkward situation. The Division may well be proud of its latest achievement."

On the 17th the battalion was relieved and found its losses consisted of 2 officers, Lieuts. J. Eadie and D. Simpson, killed, 5 officers wounded, 57 other ranks killed, 7 missing, and 69 wounded.

During the Chemical Works attack of 15th May 1916, 2nd Lieut. J. Innes with a small party of the battalion was attached to a tunnelling company to help them in their work. The tunnelling company is usually composed of quiet, sedate individuals whose duty consists in making those wonderful tunnels which in very dangerous areas take the place of communication trenches, and, when these are not required, they are employed in making dug-outs.

On this occasion, a party of 60 of them, along with Lieut. Innes and his party, were busily engaged making dug-outs in a trench some little distance behind the Chemical Works, when the enemy came in about 200 yards in front.

Lieut. Innes marshalled his battalion party, and ordered the tunnellers to stop work, and get ready to fight. As the tunnellers had few or no rifles he scoured the area round, and soon found enough derelict rifles and bayonets to arm the lot. Then over they went with fixed bayonets, and helped to rout the Boche, the worthy Lieutenant leading the way in his burberry, with his walking-stick in his hand (he thought he had come out for a peaceful night's work).

The tunnellers suffered a number of casualties, and, on their returning to their headquarters, Lieut. Innes was severely reprimanded by the Tunnellers' O.C., who told him that any one of the four sergeants he had lost was a much more valuable man to the British Army than an infantry subaltern, thus showing the high value some non-combatant corps put on their services as compared to the men who won the war.

My old château in Fampoux got a rude shock on 15th and 16th May.

Some over-daring gunners had a few days previously placed their batteries all round the house, principally in the garden and behind the garden wall, but got such a strafing that they had to change position. However, they left about three or four thousand shells, partly gas, partly high explosive, just behind the house.

On the afternoon of the 15th, a Boche shell landed in one of these stacks (the gas shell one), and off went the whole with a tremendous crash, leaving a crater 40 feet in diameter and about 15 feet deep, and for several hours thereafter the air was full of bursting shells, as the shell boxes burned merrily away.

The old château rocked under the concussion, all the slates rattled off, the gables bulged out, and even the cellar roof, strong though it was, developed a crack. For four hours the men worked in the cellar with gas masks on.

Next morning another shell put off the next dump with the result that all around is a sea of craters, while one can now sit at the foot of the cellar stairs and look up into the clear blue sky, so much of the back wall of the house has vanished.

From 17th to 30th May the battalion lay in reserve in Arras, but on that date it moved by motor-bus to Averdoingt, a quiet village far to the rear.

The month of June was spent in various quiet villages

resting and training, half the month in Eperlecques, but every move was in a northerly direction, and on 4th July the battalion moved into the St. Julien sector, two miles north of Ypres. After a four days' tour of duty in order to become familiar with the ground of the proposed offensive, they were again relieved and moved by train and route march to Lederzelle and district. Here they remained until 24th July practising the attack, and then moved to a camp in the Poperinghe area, whence by companies they went into their battle sector on the 28th, 29th and 30th.

THIRD BATTLE OF YPRES, 31ST JULY 1917

The Divisional front here lay nearly a mile east of the Yser canal, and just south of us we can see the remains of Ypres which daily gets an undue proportion of the heaviest shells the enemy can fling at it.

The canal, once busy with traffic, is now a succession of dirty stagnant pools crossed at frequent intervals by high wooden bridges for horse traffic and by low-lying bridges, supported on floating beer barrels, for pedestrians, while here and there it has been filled up with great earthen mounds, the high banks of the canal have been levelled, and on these earthen bridges rails have been laid, and at night little trucks, drawn by oil engines, pull supplies across. A bigger mound than the others has also been prepared (and has also to be repaired every day) for the broad-gauge railway line which it is intended to carry forward if the advance is a success.

One bridge is built on a little iron steamer stuck in the mud at right angles to the bridge, while the central support is a big barge half sunk in the pool.

If the builders after the war patch up the Maria Anna I. and make her fit for puffing along the canal, her sides will rival the finest patchwork quilt ever made by our grandmothers.

Here as soil, we have a dirty blue clay where water is met at 3 or 4 feet. The result is that trenches have to be built up instead of being dug down, and it is impossible to make deep dug-outs unless a pump is kept going almost continuously. The ordinary dug-out here is therefore a built-up structure, depending for safety on rows of logs or steel bars with some feet of earth and sand-bags on top, and is absolutely useless against direct hits.

The canal banks are full of these shelters and an unlucky direct hit on one of them has been known to cause one of our battalions a loss of 20 killed and 10 wounded. The west bank which is higher and stronger has a tunnel extending along it for some miles with rooms at frequent intervals, and the population in this rabbit warren generally amounts to two or three thousand men. Further north, the canal is a veritable boundary, for the enemy line swings down and runs along its eastern bank with the British on the western side.

Crossing the canal in our sector is no easy task, for the bridges are all marked by the enemy, and he is persistently shelling these and the banks in general.

The usual way is to wait some hundred yards from the canal until a lull in the shelling, and then, throwing dignity to the winds, getting across as hard as you possibly can, and taking cover in the trenches on the eastern side, or away along the roads or tracks to the rear. In the Ypres sector the farms are not grouped in villages as at Arras, but stand like our own, each in its own land. The British war-maps have named these for handy reference, and there are such names as Lancashire, Foch, Turco, Burnt and Highland Farms in our own lines, while Below, Hindenburg, Minty, Gournier, Jolie, Rudolph and Francois Farms inside the enemy lines mark points where the fiercest fighting of the advance took place, for the wily Boche had strengthened the crumbling brick walls of these farms with 3 or 4 feet of reinforced concrete, and also roofed them in, so that what, to the observer, seemed a harmless farm ruin was really a well-masked concrete redoubt which could generally withstand a direct hit unless of heavy calibre, while in the walls were steel shuttered loopholes from which, when required, the deadly machine gun could be turned on to the advancing waves.

In addition, he had numerous " pill-boxes," square or oblong forts of powerful concrete, scattered all over the area, commanding every avenue of advance.

The country is gently undulating, with occasional sluggish streams and many ditches and marshes. The German front line occupied the top of the crest and looked down on the British lines, with the Canal and country behind. The highest point of the ridge, called by us " High Command Redoubt," was a veritable cluster of pill-boxes, 20 or 30 of which were within an area of a few acres, and from these he watched all our movements and directed his batteries on to any particular point in our lines.

The night of 30th–31st July was a lovely summer night, calm and still, and until 3.50 a.m. all was quiet. At that hour, however, with a tremendous crash, every gun along the whole 15-mile-front opened out, and the noise was deafening. After an hour's intensive preparation, barrage fire was put on the enemy's front line, and over went the infantry.

The advance went like clockwork, his first, second and third defensive systems being captured up to schedule times. By the afternoon 700 prisoners had been passed back by our Division, while at least three field guns and many machine guns were captured.

Our battalion attacked on the right of the Divisional front with the 8th Argylls on their left, " A " Company capturing the German front and support line with

very little resistance. " B " Company, following
50 yards behind, captured the German reserve trench
and switch line, while two platoons of " C " Company,
passing through " B " Company, captured Sandown
and Welsh Farms, two particularly strong redoubts
behind the reserve trench.

These objectives were captured early in the forenoon, and the rest of the day was spent in con-
solidation, and remaking of roads across no-man's
land.

The battalion was withdrawn from the line on
1st August, its total casualties being 1 officer wounded,
23 other ranks killed, 9 missing and 118 wounded, very
slight casualties for such a stiff proposition as the
main trench systems of the Ypres Salient.

It was a fine sight about 6 a.m. on the morning of
the attack to watch our 18-pounder batteries go
galloping forward across the open, the six or eight
horse teams dashing across shell-holes or ditches to
take up the forward positions already settled on.
Pack horses by hundreds carrying shells, ammunition,
rations, etc., also went forward while several labour
battalions were already hard at work, almost shoulder
to shoulder, repairing the shattered roads, and carrying
the railways across our old front line into what till
that morning had been German territory. That
evening, however, the Devil was again good to his own,
for the rain came on and poured steadily for days,

making quagmires of the cross-country tracks and so delaying the advance.

Next day he counter-attacked in force, but from our Division he got it swift and heavy, and retired in confusion.

August was spent in camps in the vicinity of Poperinghe, and on the 21st, at School Camp, St. Janster-Biezen, the Commander-in-Chief, Field-Marshal Sir Douglas Haig, inspected the 152nd Infantry Brigade and expressed himself as well satisfied with the appearance of the men on parade.

On the 29th the battalion was once again in the same old rabbit warren in the Yser Canal bank, preparatory to taking over the line which was practically where we had left it a month before, our front being nearly a mile beyond the Steenbeck, a stream about 10 feet wide with marshy ground on either side, which had troubled us greatly in our first advance. On 2nd September they relieved the 6th Seaforths in this area.

At this time the Division was greatly annoyed by the activities of the enemy in Pheasant trench, a strong position with concrete blockhouses and a fortified farm called Pheasant Farm in rear. These positions were a hornet's nest of machine gunners and snipers, so it was resolved to clear them out if possible. To " D " Company under Capt. Corrigall was allotted the task, and 100 men of that Company, divided into three groups, advanced under an artillery and Stokes mortar barrage at 7.30 on the morning of the 6th. All the groups made most gallant efforts to enter Pheasant trench, but found the task beyond them, being held up, partly by uncut wire, and partly by accurate machine-gun and rifle fire and bombs from the trench and blockhouses behind. They were therefore compelled to retire after getting to within 30 yards of their objective. So heavy was the enemy fire that 50 per cent of the party became casualties, and the remainder had to lie in shell-holes until nightfall, or all would have been picked off.

Lieut. Bartleman was killed and the other two officers in charge of groups were wounded, but as showing that headquarters recognised that every effort had been made to gain the objective, Sergt. A. Mackay was awarded the D.C.M. and Sergts. J. Mowat, D.C.M., and J. Sinclair the M.M.

During this raid, Sergt. Sinclair gave the Boche an exhibition step or two of the Highland Fling. When within 60 or 70 yards of the trench, he was beckoned to approach and surrender by three Germans with a machine gun. They, judging no doubt from what they themselves would have done, thought that the added inducement of the machine gun would have brought him to their arms. However, he ignored their invitation and continued on his way from shell-hole to shell-hole, when suddenly over came a Stokes bomb which wiped machine gun and gunners out of existence. The intrepid Jimmie, on seeing this, was so charmed that he stood up and did a step of the Highland Fling (probably it was more of a war dance) in the open in full view of both parties.

By 20th September our arrangements being complete, over went the Division, carrying the line another mile forward.

There was scarcely a hitch, although the country was studded with pill-boxes big and little. Some of the smaller of these hold from 12 to 20 men, while the larger can hold from 100 upwards, and as the walls and roofs are 5 or 6 feet thick of concrete, reinforced with heavy steel girders and rails, it is no exaggeration to say that even a 6-inch shell has been seen to make a direct hit on the roof of one of these and scatter in fragments, leaving only a slight dent in the surface.

However, we brought up some of our wonderful " flying pigs," fine fat monsters, 200 pounds in weight, fired by our best trench mortars and a few of these helped very materially to alter the situation, for, even when the pill-box stood the shock, the concussion was so great that the men inside were either killed or rendered unconscious.

The battalion did not take part in the attack, its Brigade being in support, but the following night two companies took over Pheasant trench, at last in our hands, and the following night they were holding the new line where they successfully resisted most determined counter-attacks.

All these efforts were utter failures, and here the rifle found it was coming into its own again, for it helped materially to check these attacks. Five Prussian regiments took part in the attack on our Divisional front, and suffered heavy losses, for in some places his dead were piled up four or five tier deep, ranging from the bottom tier of the rather smelly variety who had been killed by our artillery some days before, to the top rows killed in the attack itself.

On 24th September we were relieved by the 6th Yorks. Regt. and proceeded to Siege Camp. On the 30th we bade farewell to the Ypres salient, hoping never to see it again, and entrained for Achiet Le Petit, a village five miles north-west of Bapaume, where we arrived at 4 a.m. on 1st October.

THE HENINEL SECTOR, OCTOBER 1917

After six days in Achiet le Petit, a move was made to Mercatel where battalion training went on until the 14th. Another move took us to Henin camp just behind the line, where for eight days we supplied working parties, until, on the 22nd, we took over from the 6th Seaforths the line in front of Heninel about six miles south-east of Arras, where we remained until the 31st, when we went back to a familiar camp, Y huts on the Arras-St. Pol road.

The change from muddy shell-holes, dirty pill-boxes, and no definite trench line, from incessant artillery fire and heavy aerial bombing, to this quiet, delectable spot where shells seldom trouble one, where aeroplanes are at a minimum, where there are excellent trenches and splendid, deep, dry dug-outs, all constructed by the Boche for the Boche, but now used by us, is a glorious one, for which all ranks are truly grateful.

This is the country from which the Boche had to fall back last spring as his position had become untenable. It is an undulating, farming country, dotted with numerous villages of the farming type. The Boche had held this area since 1914, and except for those who had fled before him, the remainder of the inhabitants had lived in servitude ever since, forced to cultivate their land and then have the greater part of their produce seized by the enemy, leaving them just enough to eke out a miserable existence on. He dwelt in their houses, ordered them about, bullied and ill-used them, demanded the first and best of everything, and compelled them to help to dig his trenches and dug-outs.

This country, 70 miles long, varying in width from 30 miles of a maximum, tapering to a mile or two at the northern extremity, is now in our hands, but what a country! Prior to leaving, the Boche drove the surviving inhabitants back before him, removed all their horses and cattle, and then deliberately placed bombs inside the village houses and blew them to smithereens. There is scarcely a shell-hole to be seen around here, so that these houses were not destroyed by shell-fire, but one can plainly see they have been blown outwards, in fact one can, in many cases, see the craters in the floors made by the bombs.

For the time being we are in huts beside a village which in peace times must have held five or six hundred inhabitants. On the outside of the village was a nice mansion house or château. All that now remains of it are the pillars at the entrance to the drive. The house itself had been so completely destroyed that it was simply a heap of bricks and chalk, the bricks being so broken up by the explosion that they were only fit for road-making. This countryside was noted for its woods, every road having on either side a row of magnificent trees, many of them 3 or 4 feet in diameter, while every village was embowered in its grove, and trees were dotted among the farms. Being a good country for fruit, each village had splendid orchards growing apples, pears, plums, etc. The dirty Boche before he left must have employed thousands of men cutting down these trees, and now all that remains are the rows of stumps with the fallen trees lying alongside. As far as the eye can see there is not a tree to be seen, except at the little cemetery beside which he buried his own dead, and even there he removed the fence from around the French cemetery and put it around his own. With the low cunning of his race, he took care to bury one or two British and French soldiers, probably prisoners who had succumbed to wounds, among his own, so that the graves of his dead might be saved from being ploughed over after the war.

The only tree I saw standing in one large area was a fine weeping willow, which, with sardonic humour, he left alone while the grove around was levelled.

I can count thirteen villages (or rather what is left of them) in our Divisional area, villages which before the war must have held populations varying from 200 to 1500, and now scarcely one stone is left upon another.

Some of the French refugees who fled further into France in 1914 are beginning to creep back here to try and pick up the broken threads of their old life. A pitiable sight it is to see old men and women coming up in farm carts to their native village and to note the look of anguish and despair on their faces when they see what is left of it.

Still, some wonderful things happen. Two old ladies came toddling up the other day, got the loan of eight or nine of our soldiers, located at last their old house and selected a particular spot in what was once the garden. After the soldiers had removed the heaps of brick and stone and dug further down a tin box was turned up, containing in this case 1000 francs and in another similar case 2000, roughly £40 and £80 respectively, the family nest eggs which they had buried before they fled, and which had escaped the Boche. Another party was not so successful for they failed to find what they had hidden. The French Government are taking a paternal interest in these poor sufferers, and already near here I have seen a Government house made of blocks of concrete in sections, with a tiled roof, buildings which look very neat and serviceable, and which can be erected very quickly.

Our own Army also assists, and puts on as many men as can be spared to plough and sow. Hundreds of acres just behind have already been ploughed, mostly with motor tractors, so that what has been unproductive for three years will next year once again be giving.

The weather all October has been very changeable, a dry day or two, then heavy rains come on, but the roads are good, deep dug-outs and our own shelters are plentiful, and the only worry our men have is from the Boche trench-mortars, minenwerfers, and spring-bombs which annoy our front line at times, but even in this department he gets more than he gives.

The Cambrai Offensive, November 1917

While the battalions were resting in the vicinity of Arras, advance parties were sent up to prepare for the new offensive, in which we hoped to break through the Hindenburg line and capture Cambrai. To the 51st Division was allocated the task of breaking the line in front of Trescault, striking at the strongly fortified villages of Flesquieres, Cantaing and Fontaine-Notre Dame, the latter village lying almost on the eastern edge of the famous Bourlon Wood.

As a member of one of these advance parties, it was my unlucky fate to forego the quiet pleasures of Y huts, Maroeuil, and such pleasant abodes, and to find myself in October dumped in the remains of Metz, a village just behind Havrincourt Wood and close to our new front.

When we arrived on the scene, we were greeted by the Ulster Division then holding the line with the exclamation " Burds of Ill Omen," and on our professing to be quiet wanderers, spying out the land, we were told that our appearance in that peaceful countryside denoted there was something in the wind, so we said nothing. In Metz, I celebrated my third birthday—in France—and " at present I am living at a farm "— and a proper Bairnsfather farm it is, in one of the Hun-blown-up villages I have already described. The only habitations the Boche did not blow up in this village were one house and all the village pig-sties. As to the latter, I expect a brotherly feeling towards the former occupants of these little abodes prevented him from wreaking vengeance on their domiciles. The solitary standing house was the headquarters of the Commandant, and was left to the last moment for His Hunship's comfort. It was meant to be blown up, for our men found an unexploded bomb in the cellar. Otherwise the village was blown to smithereens.

Early in October " Robin " and " Mac " set off with ten trusty men and true to see about preparing telephone lines, preparatory to the aforesaid "show." For the first night poor " Robin " and " Mac " shared a pig-sty, and the ten men had half a stable, the upper part having been blown clean away, leaving, providentially, an arched brick ceiling over their heads. Coming up a day later we flitted into this farm with a big tarpaulin as a rain-proof over what remains of the original roof, which is not much. In one day we all had beds (old beams and wire-netting make grand beds, I may say). We had fire-places of bricks, and, as for firewood, we had what lay on the ground of the village trees, and all its scattered beams and couples.

So the preparatory work went merrily on, until the Clerk of the Weather suddenly turned very nasty, and poured down the vials of his liquid wrath upon us. The tarpaulin, we found, was largely, as we had laid it, a delusion and a snare, " Robin " gathering two tin basins of water off his bed between 5 and 9 p.m., and on arising next morning from his clammy couch he found everything soaked through and through.

" Mac " and I providentially had our beds in corners

where the idiosyncrasies of the tarpaulin's convoluted form prevented the rain from entering except in minor quantities, and we were comparatively dry. However, as we had the biggest and hottest fire of logs in France, we and our belongings were soon dry, although my steel helmet which had been hanging by its strap, basin-fashion, had collected a good deal of moisture and required some extra heat before being again fit to wear. The boys, trusting to their arched brick roof, had made no overhead arrangements, with the result that the ever inquisitive raindrops found the weak joints in the arched brick armour, and pelted down upon them, with the result that " Still " had to leave his bed and sleep under the rustic table they had made, which acted as a rain-screen for him, and " Forbie " erected a waterproof sheet over his bed, slanting, so that the water ran down it, just finding the floor beyond where his toes were.

Our dining-room was absolutely the limit. Having dug an old French stove for it out of the ruins, and lifted it in, we thought we were complete, but between the awful smoke from the stove which would not vent, and the persistent drip from the roof, we had at last to vacate the dining-room until better weather conditions prevailed.

Two or three of the boys, realizing that it was better to be dry in a pig-sty than wet in a stable, promptly reverted to the pig-sties, and by the third day of steady rain were able to talk in a rather superior way to the bedraggled denizens of the stable and farm.

My birthday was rather a quiet affair, as we were working too hard for formal birthday parties, and then the 13th of November was looming in the immediate future, but Coullie, Hunter and Will looked in from the artillery to wish me many happy returns, and we burned at least another cartload of old rafters over their visit.

The 13th of November, the anniversary of Beaumont-Hamel, that victory which really forced the Boche to make his retirement, was celebrated in great style by the Division. Wherever work permitted, there was a holiday for all, with football matches, etc., the usual rations were supplemented for the day, horse races and sports were held, and generally, as the Division was out of the line training, the men had a free day and a good time.

By this time our numbers had increased to 30, as men were being gradually sent up to us. Each little party of four or five on arrival was greeted with the announcement that there was still a vacant pig-sty, at which some looked rather perturbed, especially the redoubtable Strain, cleverest and best of telephone experts. However, after he and his three men had taken their double pig-sty in hand, within four hours they had converted the two into one, by pulling down the brick partition, had built a fireplace and erected beds, and

185

had found a shattered door somewhere. They were then very comfortable indeed, and looked with disdain on the dripping comfort of the stable. That enlarged pig-sty when the French return must, unless altered again, be used for some old mother pig and family, as it is now too large for one solitary " Sanny Cammell."

The morning of 20th November opened dull but dry. During the previous days there was very little firing on either side, but guns were being quietly brought up at night, while millions of rounds of ammunition were also stacked at battery positions and carefully camouflaged so that no hostile aeroplane could possibly notice any difference. By 4 a.m. the tanks, scores of them, were at our front line, and so also were our own gallant fellows, ready for the newest venture in the war —a battle without any previous artillery preparation, without any smashing by shell-fire of the wide stretching zones of barbed wire in front of the Boche trenches, an attack which might be a great success and which might equally well be a great failure.

The conditions were as follows : Our front line lay on the top of a rounded grassy ridge, while in the valley below, over 1000 yards away, was the Boche front line system consisting of three parallel rows of trenches with five or six lines of barbed wire in front of the first, each line being 5 to 10 yards wide, and consisting of a perfect maze of jagged wire fixed on iron posts driven into the ground. Between the three trenches

were other stretches of barbed wire, while there were
many 30-foot dug-outs in each trench. Beyond
this formidable system lay the village of Ribecourt on
the further slope of the valley, a maze of concrete dug-
outs, machine-gun emplacements and trenches. Behind that again, and further up the slope, was the
Boche second system of defence, consisting of two parallel trenches with more heavy barbed wire in front,
and here our objective was the village of Flesquieres,
on the highest part of the ridge. Further on the slope
ran down to Cantaing, rising again towards Fontaine,
with Bourlon Wood and village on the left.

At 6.20 a.m. after a quiet and almost silent night, the
tanks crossed our front line, waddled through our own
wire, and then proceeded across an almost unshelled
and grassy downward slope towards the Boche front
line. Each lumbering monster flattened out in his track
all the barbed wire he crossed over, leaving a path
9 or 10 feet wide, still rather prickly with the flattened wire, but quite passable, wherever they crossed.
Some had dragging behind, on long chains, what might
be called for want of a better term four-pronged
anchors, and when these caught in a stretch of barbed
wire and the tanks went on, scores of yards with iron
posts and all complete followed, and the twisted up mass
was dropped at one side, leaving a clear way of advance.

Allowing the tanks a start of one or two hundred
yards the first wave of infantry followed, and were soon

in the first Boche trench. By this time the Boche knew something was on, for one cannot silence a tank engine, but with the exception of some machine-gunners all retired to their deep dug-outs and surrendered *en masse*. Two companies of our own battalion took part in the first wave which "mopped up" the first system of trenches, while the other two went across in the second wave, pressing on towards Ribecourt and Flesquieres.

So sure were some of our own men of success that one of them went across with a canvas water bucket hung round his neck to collect souvenirs from the Boche prisoners and dug-outs; and I understand the bucket was well filled before the morning was far advanced.

Ribecourt was captured in spite of its strong defences with scarcely a struggle, the battalion having hardly a dozen casualties in this advance of 1½ mile, while the prisoners taken by the battalion amounted to about 300, including a number of officers. Four field-guns were also captured by the battalion, the gunners scuttling for dear life before the kilted advance. The other battalions in the Division did equally well, and soon crowds of Boche prisoners were trekking to the rear to the cages prepared for them.

To show how unexpected was our attack we captured in the valley to the left of Ribecourt a Boche cooker, a kind of four-wheeled iron waggon with a fire and boilers, in which hot meals are cooked and brought up near the trenches. The first wave pounced upon the waggon with the horses yoked and the Boche dinner cooking away merrily, but the driver elected to run away, much to his own detriment, for he did not run far. The morning air had created a keen appetite among the members of this Company, and right heartily did they tackle that hot meal of beef and vegetables which the cooker contained. Some aver that the so-called beef was horse-flesh, but, horse-flesh or not, it was very acceptable on that cold winter morning, and the cooker was soon empty, and thereafter brought back by the two Boche horses, but with a British driver, to the " Fifth's " transport lines.

The majority of the tanks were still pushing merrily ahead, although a few had broken down, and Ribe-court having been disposed of early in the morning the next wave followed the tanks towards the Flesquieres slope, where the second barbed wire system and trenches confronted us. This was a much more difficult position to attack as the village looked down on the slopes up which our men had to advance.

Our battalion's objective on the first day was the railway line just below the slope, and this they reached 2 hours 50 minutes after the attack began, in which time they had captured four lines of trenches, while their total casualties were one officer wounded, four other ranks killed and 20 wounded.

The attack on Flesquieres was held up on the first

day, mainly by the gallant conduct of a German artillery warrant-officer, who rallied his gunners to their anti-tank gun, knocked out four of the tanks whose duty it was to smash the barbed wire in front of the village and thus prevented the infantry from getting forward.

It was on this day that L/Corpl. R. Macbeath won the V.C.

On the western outskirts of Ribecourt was a system of deep dug-outs with a strong machine post in front, a post which effectually swept our own advancing troops as well as the 1st Leicestershire Regiment on our right.

L/Corpl. Macbeath's heroic deed is thus described in the *London Gazette* of 11th January 1918.

Awarded the Victoria Cross

For most conspicuous bravery when with his company in attack and approaching the final objective. A nest of enemy machine guns in the western outskirts of a village opened fire, both on his own unit and on the unit on the right. The advance was checked, and heavy casualties resulted.

When a Lewis gun was called for, to deal with these machine guns, L/Corpl. Macbeath volunteered for the duty, and immediately moved off alone with a Lewis gun and his revolver. He located one of the guns in action, and worked his way towards it, shooting the gunner with his revolver at 20 yards range. Finding several other hostile machine guns in action, he, with the assistance of a tank, attacked them and drove the gunners to ground in a deep dug-out.

L/Corpl. Macbeath, regardless of all danger, rushed in after them, shot an enemy who opposed him on the steps, and drove the remainder of the garrison out of the dug-out, capturing three officers and thirty men.

There were in all five machine guns mounted round the dug-out, and by putting them out of action he cleared the way for the advance of both units.

The conduct of L/Corpl. Macbeath throughout three days of severe fighting was beyond praise.

On the morning of the 21st the battalion formed up on the railway at 6.10 a.m., and advanced on Flesquieres which they found abandoned, so they pushed on towards Cantaing, a village 1½ miles further on, and by 9.30 a.m. they had gained their objective, again with slight losses, namely, one officer wounded, one other rank killed and 13 wounded.

The 154th Brigade then pushed on and captured Cantaing and Fontaine also with comparatively little resistance.

The infantry were now at the top of the rise and looking right down upon Cambrai, the great Hindenburg line had been completely broken, and, according to prearranged plans the cavalry and horse artillery should now have entered the fight and swept down upon the town.

It was a fine sight to see an apparently endless succession of men and horses wending their way across the valley towards Ribecourt and Flesquieres, but to the infantrymen it was a maddening sight to see them come wending back next morning having accomplished nothing. True, two squadrons went round Cambrai, and did some damage on the way, but the remainder of the 27,000 cavalry we had heard so much about did nothing, while some batteries of Royal Horse Artillery were still in their original positions behind the British front line when the Field Artillery were 3 or 4 miles into the German lines. However, what could one expect when the antediluvian fossil in charge of one sector of the cavalry front knew so little about modern warfare that on coming to occupy as his battle headquarters a dug-out in the British front line, a dug-out which was also the cable-head of that front, he ordered the signal corporal and sapper in charge of the terminal board out of the dug-out, having seemingly never seen or heard of such innovations as buried or ground cables in his life before.

After Fontaine had been captured, the Boche seemed to realize that we were out for breaking his line, so he poured out of Cambrai two Divisions against this one village at the time held by two Companies of the 4th Seaforths. On they came, line after line, and our

Lewis gunners and riflemen had the time of their lives. Swathes of men were mown down, lanes were cut through his closely massed formations, and yet so numerous were they that by sheer weight of numbers they recaptured the village, forcing the survivors of the 4th Seaforths to fall back on our next line.

On the 23rd we attacked again, but by that time Fontaine was a nest of machine guns and rifles, and the only way to recapture it was to turn the heavies on to it and raze it to the ground, which has since been done. In this attack, we lost one other rank killed and 19 wounded, or a total of two officers wounded, six other ranks killed, and 52 wounded for four days' continuous fighting.

On the second day of the battle fell dear old E. A. Mackintosh, the author of *A Highland Regiment* and *War; the Liberator*, familiarly known as "Tosh," poet, *littérateur*, and hail-fellow-well-met to one and all. His happy smile and cheery personality will long be remembered by us, while his topical songs often cheered us on our way. Of a truly poetic temperament, he laughed away all troubles, and helped to cheer even the most lugubrious members of the battalion by his humour and fun. And yet beneath it all he had a very sympathetic heart. I remember at the time of the raid for which he won the M.C., after he had helped to carry in the wounded, how he broke down and wept bitterly because after carrying one of his wounded men for over 100 yards through the Boche trenches, with the Boche following close behind, he had to abandon him at the enemy front line, the man dying of his wounds when they had hoisted him out of the trench. Kind and cheerful under all circumstances, his men loved him and would do anything for him. Now he rests in his last long sleep among his men in a little cemetery in Orival Wood, and the Division, and even his country, are the poorer by his being cut off in the springtime of his youth.

On the 24th the battalion was relieved by a unit of the Guards' Division which had been lying 10 or 12 miles behind, and had been wondering if its existence had been entirely forgotten by the higher powers, seeing they had left the tired troops of the Highland Division to fight away by themselves on such an important front and at such a crucial time, while fresh troops like the Guards were itching to be in the fray. By train and route march, rest camp at Senlis behind Albert was reached on the 25th and every one settled down for a good time. Here some of the old-timers were delighted to have a visit from Col. Davidson who was in command during our first year in France, and who was now Agricultural Officer of the Third Army.

Suddenly on the 30th word came that the Germans had made a smashing attack and had broken through our lines in front of Gouzeaucourt, with the result that the Division was hurried up in support, and the Fifth found themselves that evening in Barastre Camp just behind their former front. It was intended that we should take over our old front here, but as matters had improved by this time, mainly owing to the heroic efforts of the Guards, we were moved further north, and took over the sector through which runs the main Bapaume-Cambrai road.

On 4th December the battalion took over the line east of the village of Boursies. Since the November attack, our front line in this sector has been the old German front line, but as there was no advantage to be gained by holding this, owing to our retiral further south, it was resolved to retire to our own old front line, which was done on the night of the 4th–5th without a casualty. It was rare fun next morning to see the enemy energetically bombarding his own old front line where not a single man of ours remained.

To the " Fifth " fell part of the duty of making the enemy's re-entry into his old front line as troublesome and expensive as possible.

Two sections of " D " Company under Lieut. Shaw remained for two days and nights in an old trench in no-man's land, during which time they greatly harassed the enemy, killing and wounding a goodly number as he came forward, carefully feeling his way for traps.

For his gallant work in this party, Sergt. Hugh Matheson received the D.C.M. Running short of bombs and seeing some Mills grenades lying in the open in front, he went out under heavy fire and brought in 20, which saved the post from being rushed during the next attack. He himself personally accounted for seven of the enemy.

Then a night or two later Lieut. Marks with a small party attacked a group of houses in front from which we had been annoyed by machine-gun fire, and thoroughly scuppered a German patrol which was in occupancy. Surrounding a house, our men ordered the inmates to surrender. One man, after holding up his hands, drew his revolver and shot Sergt. MacKenzie. Needless to say, he did not get a chance to repeat his treachery, and several of his comrades also paid for his breach of faith.

From the 11th to the 22nd the battalion was in reserve at Fremicourt, and Christmas and New Year were celebrated in camp at Beugny and Lebucquiere respectively.

The New Year was ushered in with the usual Highland éclat. As soon as midnight came the pipe-bands of the various Highland regiments around struck up a merry tune, and by the cheering which arose one could judge that the majority of those in the locality had not yet gone to bed. A goodly amount of first-footing also took place, and we learned at least one new first-footing custom, when "Texas Pete," an attached doctor from "God's own country," first-footed us and insisted on bringing into our hut a ladder which he said was always carried in his country when first-footing, but why, he did not explain.

The only exciting incident of the latter half of the month was a visit we had from a squadron of Boche bombing aeroplanes. It was a bright moonlit night, and early in the evening the whir of aeroplane engines was heard, and then the bombs began to crash. He must have had a big squadron out, probably 15 to 20 machines, and as each carries nine or more bombs, the din was terrific. It was not exactly a pleasurable experience to sit in a tent or tin hut with nowhere else to go, and hear that monotonoüs whir come nearer and nearer until you calculate it is overhead or nearly so, and then listen to the crash, crash, crash, as the Boche releases one bomb after the other, and they come smashing all around you while you speculate, as you hear the swish of the falling bomb, whether it is to get your abode or not. The only thing is to lie as flat as possible with all lights out and hope for the best, but when some jocular member of the party, on hearing the whir removing itself, starts playing on a tin whistle " Will ye no' come back again ? " you want to throw something at his head, as your wishes certainly don't agree with the sentiments of that Jacobite ballad.

Next morning, however, every man was digging like fury, every group of huts or tents busy on the construction of bomb-proof shelters alongside, so that on another visit every one could pop into these shelters and have above his head enough beams, corrugated iron and earth to nullify the effects of any aeroplane bomb. By the next moonrise all the members of our Company had some rabbit hole to pop into should occasion arise, and an air of security reigned over our camp.

CHAPTER V

THE 1918 CAMPAIGN

THE GERMAN OFFENSIVE, 21ST MARCH 1918

Maybe that we shall drive them,
Maybe we fight in vain,
We care not now our fathers
Are born in us again.
When the old voices called us
We heard them and obeyed,
Whether we die or conquer
We have not been afraid.

E. A. MACKINTOSH, M.C.

JANUARY, February and early March were passed in the usual round of trench warfare—reserve, support, and line in turn—and the names of Lebucquiere, Boursies, Louverval, Achiet-le-Grand, Beugny and Fremicourt recall what on the whole was a quite pleasant part of the line.

Fatigues were heavy, however, as the long expected German offensive was bound to be near, so the 51st Division worked practically night and day, improving the existing trenches, digging the new Beaumetz-Morchies line, with new communication and switch trenches, and closing the front and each system with miles upon miles of barbed wire, while at the same time making an elaborate buried telephone cable system from 6 to 8 feet deep, extending almost from the front line well back towards the Divisional Headquarters at Fremicourt.

If every Division on this front had been as well dug-in and wired-in as ours, the enemy would never have broken the line, but when one Division puts forward every effort to make things secure, while the next on the right or left is allowed to take things in easy fashion, or devotes its work parties to the less essential, it is evident that the chain will snap at its weakest link, and so it was in March, the weak links then being those Divisions which had not worked systematically all the spring at defensive works, while in April the weak link was the Portuguese Corps sandwiched in the middle of the British line.

The weather on the whole was splendid, so different from that of our spring offensive in 1917, and if the old proverb that the " deil's bairns hae their faither's luck " is true the Boche must be highly favoured bairns of his Satanic Majesty, for the weather did suit their preparatory arrangements as it never suited ours.

On the morning of the 21st March our three battalions, the 5th and 6th Seaforths and 6th Gordons, were in the line practically astride the Bapaume-Cambrai main road which runs " straight as a die " from one town to the other. Our own battalion's front lay across this road which we knew the Boche would use more than any other in his expected advance.

Our battalion was the left battalion of the centre Brigade. On our left was a Brigade of Black Watch and Gordons, while on our right was a Brigade of Seaforths and Gordons. Further on our left was the 6th Division. At 5 a.m. to the minute, after a quiet night, every gun on the German front opened with most terrific fire. Guns of all calibres opened out as hard as they could fire, the front lines being heavily barraged, whilst his heavies systematically shelled support and reserve lines and billeting areas far in the rear. Thousands of guns must have been massed for his great offensive.

After five hours of this systematic and devastating shelling, his infantry advanced to the attack, masses upon masses of men pouring forward towards the British front line. It is reckoned that nine German Divisions attacked our Divisional front alone; while in guns he must have had ten to one. And yet so systematically had our Division dug itself in, working steadily since it took over this part of the line, so strong were we closed in with barbed wire, and so strong were our trenches and posts, that he utterly failed to break through our front, in spite of his masses of men and his weight of artillery.

What disturbed our men a great deal was his gas

shells, with which he deluged our front, support, and reserve trenches, but, through gas curtains over the doors of dug-outs and box respirators on the men, there were few casualties from this. With such heavy fire, all telephone cables in the forward area were soon blown to atoms, and the battalion had to depend largely on runners for keeping in touch with other battalions and the Brigade. These did excellent work, going out time and again with their dispatches, and generally getting through to their destination in spite of the most terrific barrage we have ever experienced.

By 9 a.m. our front trenches were practically wiped out, yet the enemy hesitated to attack frontally. He had more success, however, further on our left, breaking through the 6th Division and forcing our left Brigade, the 153rd, to swing back its left flank to prevent us being cut off. The first our battalion saw of attacking troops was on their left flank, crossing the Louverval Ridge where two of our Lewis gunners did excellent work, firing 1000 rounds each at him as he advanced in massed formation, inflicting heavy casualties.

As the Boche came on on the left and threatened to cut the battalion off by working round our rear, the men of our right front company (the left front company was practically wiped out) slowly retired to a village called Boursies when they again stubbornly held out. From this they again fell back to another system of trenches called the intermediate line, which they held for a time, but the Boche was again on high ground on their left flank, and completely enfiladed our trenches. Here fell that gallant lad, the Adjutant of the regiment, Capt. Ian Mackenzie, one of the finest scholars and bravest officers who ever came from the north. Capt. Charles Mackay, dear old serious Charles, was also killed, while Capt. Bert Sinclair was wounded, and had to be left behind in a dug-out owing to the retiral. This sustained effort of our battalion as they stubbornly fought their way back from point to point, holding up the Boche in his determined effort to completely break through, has been described by General Haig as a " very gallant fight," for, although surrounded, they still fought on, and saved the situation.

From Boursies, they again fell back to a sunken road north of a village called Doignies, and here again, after holding out for some time, the enemy flanking movement forced them to fall back another mile to west of Hermies. From 6 p.m. to 11 p.m. of the 21st the battalion held out here and then moved again, but this time to the left, in front of Beaumetz, which line they occupied at 2 a.m. of the 22nd. Here they took over the headquarters of the Brigade which had fallen back, and held on until 7.30 p.m., suffering very few casualties although heavily shelled. They were then ordered to fall back another mile to a village called Lebucquiere where they dug a new system of trenches which were completed by daylight. During the night of the 21st, all day of the 22nd, and again on the night of the 22nd, although exhausted from lack of sleep and food, and from their strenuous exertions, they worked at digging new trenches with energy and goodwill.

From 6 to 8 o'clock on the morning of the 23rd, their new line was heavily shelled, and at 8 a.m. large numbers of the enemy advanced against what at the best was bound to be a poor trench system. Three times he came on and was hurled back by rifle and Lewis gun fire, and many casualties were inflicted upon him, but the flank gave way once again, and our men fell back to the Corps line south-west of Lebucquiere and Velu. Here they held on till 3 p.m., when, under orders, they fell back to the next defensive line near Bancourt, two miles further west. Here, reinforced by the remainder of the Fifth from Echelon B, under Lieut. Grant, they remained until the forenoon of the 24th, being intermittently shelled during that time.

In the forenoon troops from further forward, being heavily shelled, fell back through our position, and the Germans advanced. On this occasion the troops on both flanks fell back, and in spite of driving the enemy back twice the battalion had to withdraw once again. Our Brigade was by this time very depleted, many of its bravest and best having fought their last fight for the honour of old Scotland and laid down their gallant young lives for all that honourable men hold dear—

freedom and liberty. A composite battalion was here formed from the survivors of the Brigade, Echelon B of our Battalion forming " A " Company, and fell back to Loupart Wood, where once again they dug themselves in, completing a new system of trenches by midnight. To attain this position meant a march of 4½ miles and intensive digging after that, and yet the work was done. Thereafter this Company fell back and joined the remainder of the Brigade, in front of Irles, over a mile further west.

By this time the battalion was acting as supporting troops for a fresh Division which had been put in to relieve our men, now exhausted by losses and five days' lack of sleep and proper food. Yet, in spite of being fresh, the new Division broke before the overwhelming numbers of the enemy, and fell back through the battalion's position. Lieut. J. B. Simpson of our battalion here did some splendid work, for which he afterwards was awarded the M.C., attempting to rally this Division's men who were retiring in some confusion, but he found it was impossible to do so, so once again we fell back. Ammunition by this time was very short, and, as other Divisions were being brought up, and our men were utterly exhausted, the battalion fell back to Colincamps, whence it marched to Sailly-au-Bois, where they lay by the roadside and slept the first sleep they had had for six days. As the night was bitterly cold and frosty, it caused still more suffering to men who had already suffered to the limit of human endurance.

Early on the 26th the battalion was again on the march, and once more took up an outpost position, as report had it that German cavalry had broken through. After the transport got safely away, the march was resumed, and the battalion late on the evening of the 26th bivouacked in the Bois de Chatelet near Pas.

It was my duty on the morning of the 26th to march further back, a distance of 15 miles, with a party of 150 men, and on the way we came upon the find of our lives. Living on scraps of bully and dog biscuits for six days with little or no sleep, we were rather hungry, and coming to a village about half-way we halted in the square and decided to look around to see if we could get beer or bread from the French, some of whom were still there. We found still better, for in one Brigade headquarters' kitchen (the Brigade had moved rather suddenly that morning) we found a magnificent roast just done to a turn, a fine pan of rice pudding, and bread and butter galore. So we had a gorgeous feast in the old village square, and left that village looking more like old-time Scotch marauders then quiet twentieth-century fighters, for nearly all had sand-bags full of underclothes, bread, butter, etc., so that every one was, by night, clean outside and well dined inside. Truly we were far cheerier at the end of the 15-mile tramp than at the beginning.

THE 1918 CAMPAIGN

The battalion casualties in the retreat were: officers, 3 killed, 7 wounded, 3 missing; other ranks, 30 killed, 115 wounded, 219 missing. The greater proportion of the missing are now known to have been killed.

A rather curious incident happened on the second day of the battle. A little parachute, seemingly fired from a rifle, fell in our lines and was found to bear attached to it the following message:

"Good old 51st! Still sticking it. Cheerio!" Such was the message we got from some Boche with more chivalry than most of his compatriots.

On leaving this front the Army Commander sent the Division the following appreciation:

"I cannot allow the 51st Division to leave my army without expressing my appreciation of their splendid conduct during the stage of the great battle which is just completed. By their devotion and courage, they have broken up overwhelming attacks, and prevented the enemy gaining his object, namely a decisive victory. I wish them every possible good luck."

On the 29th the battalion marched to Frevent and entrained for Fouquereuil, a country village a few miles behind Bethune, where the depleted ranks were made up with drafts fresh from home.

Many a sad heart will there be in Highland and Lowland homes over this six days' battle; but this sadness should be tempered with pride at the glorious fight for freedom and right made by our Northern battalions against the powers of darkness as typified by those brutal adversaries, the Boche. Pessimistic you may be at times at home, pessimistic we may be sometimes out here, but bear in mind we are fighting for our lives, our liberties, and all we hold dear, and that, if we do not persevere to the bitter end, to the sacrificing of our last man and our last gun, our race is doomed, our past is wiped out, and we are no longer a free nation, but a race of slaves under the most cruel, vindictive, and blood-thirsty tyrants that ever tried to rule the world—a nation with no sense of honour, no sense of chivalry, no sense of decency even ; a nation which will grind us into the dust if it once gains the supremacy, and will make us wish we had never been born.

When I looked on our survivors the sixth day coming slowly back, footsore and weary, with dazed eyes—dazed from what they had come through, and from utter weariness of body and mind—when I saw our lads of 19 and 20, after putting in a most gallant fight, dropping by the roadside, utterly exhausted and done, and thought of some of those at home who think of nothing but how much money they can make out of this accursed war, I am tempted to ask if it is worth our fighting for such skunks who seem to have neither patriotism nor self-respect as long as their precious skins are safe.

THE 1918 CAMPAIGN

On 4th April a move was made to Marles-les-
Mines and thence to Manqueville where at 6 a.m.
on the 9th the alarm was sounded, and the battalion
was ordered to stand to, and then proceeded by
bus to Fosse, a village on the Lawe River, slightly
north of Vieille Chapelle, an area with which we
had been very familiar in 1915, but which we had
not visited in the interval. This front was held by a
Portuguese Division which had broken very badly
when the enemy attacked, so that by the time of our
arrival on the scene the enemy had advanced from
4 to 5 miles, his troops had passed over all our trench
systems, and were in a peaceful farming country
which had been practically undisturbed all through
the war.

The country looked beautiful. The mild March had
enabled the old farmers and their womenfolk to get
their crops down early, the winter wheat was already
3 or 4 inches high, the fruit trees were all in full blossom,
the garden seeds were bursting from the ground, some
of the trees were half in leaf, when the battalion moved
up to Fosse. This sector is quite different from the
scene of our March battle.

There, it was undulating country with slopes and
valleys, most of it was a desert with houses and

159

villages blown to pieces long before, and with no French population.

Here, the country is a great plain with water-logged ditches everywhere, and with many intersecting roads, while the farms, instead of being grouped in villages, are scattered over the country like our own at home. The French were living on their farms, the war had never touched them so far, all was a picture of rural felicity when the staggering news was brought to them that the hated Boche was upon them. Poor people! It would have required a heart of stone not to have felt sorry for them. With tears in their eyes they packed all they could of their most easily moved possessions on the farm cart, on wheelbarrows, on perambulators, and leading their cattle, set out, whither they knew not, but, as long as it was away from their detested enemy, they cared not. Streaming down the roads they came, looking the picture of despair and apathy as if their world had indeed come to an end.

No able-bodied young indispensables in that crowd. The old grandfather of 70 or over leading the horse, the younger children perched among the household Penates in the lumbering four-wheeled waggon, the women walking alongside generally carrying extra bundles on their backs and leading the cattle, with perhaps a boy of 13 or 14 wheeling a barrow behind, also loaded to its fullest capacity.

But these were the more fortunate ones. Nearer the

line, so quick was the advance of the Boche that the people had barely time to flee for their lives, and had to abandon everything, and many in their flight, who got caught between the advancing enemy and our troops coming up, undoubtedly suffered from artillery and machine-gun fire and were killed as they fled.

In one deserted farmhouse, at the time being subjected to heavy machine-gun fire, we found several cows still fastened in their stalls, pigs wandering about the farmyard, and hens galore feeding away as if the world were going on as usual.

We unfastened the cattle and drove them to the rear, but the Boche must have got them after all, as he had that farm in the afternoon.

Everywhere it was the same, cattle, pigs and fowls wandering about ownerless, while the fields, lately drilled and sown, were being torn up by shells or dug up in the making of trenches by our men in trying to stem the enemy's advance.

Some of the older people, however, refused to budge, preferring to encounter the dangers of shot and shell rather than leave the old home.

In one farmhouse occupied by a Brigade Headquarters, we found an old woman of 87 sitting placidly by the kitchen fire where the Brigade cooks were making a meal. When the rest of the family fled, she absolutely refused to budge, so they left her, and our boys did all they could to make her comfortable. To look at her, one would think she was sitting in the bosom of her own family, so calm and collected did she seem.

In another house further along we found all alone an old man of 80 determined to take what the fates would send rather than leave his all.

Quite cool he was, for when we asked for a certain farm which we wished to locate he fetched his spectacles, looked at our map, and then directed us. As both farms were in the enemy's hands after severe fighting next day, one wonders what became of them.

One of our waggons picked up an old lady of 83 stolidly marching towards her home in Robecq which was at the time on fire and being heavily shelled. Do or say what we could, nothing was of any avail, she must go to Robecq, although how she was to walk the intervening six miles was beyond us. However, we handed her over to a French interpreter and left him trying to argue her into a more reasonable frame of mind. As for the battalion, by midday of the 9th it was in action, "A" and "D" Companies reinforcing the Corps Cyclists and King Edward's Horse at Les Huit Maisons in front of the River Lawe with "B" and "C" covering the bridges over the river. Under heavy machine-gun fire "A" reached its objective, but "D" found the enemy had broken through on the left, so that it had to take up a flanking position. Here Capt. Corrigall, one of the older officers and a great favourite with all, was dangerously wounded and later died of his wounds.

Capt. Corrigall had gone forward to reconnoitre the position, taking Sergt. Hugh Matheson, D.C.M., with him. When he was wounded Sergt. Matheson bound up his wounds, and then returned to the Company, and led them to the position selected by Capt. Corrigall. He then returned for his officer, and carried him back to a place of safety under heavy machine-gun fire. Returning to the Company he did exceptionally good work during the following days, when all but one of the officers had become casualties, and was awarded the M.M. for his gallantry.

King Edward's Horse, a very gallant body of men, whom the Division had had with it on many occasions as mounted orderlies, here showed what they could do as infantry, and they and " A " Coy. kept the enemy at bay, driving him back many times with severe losses, until 6 p.m., when heavy enfilade fire forced a retiral of 300 yards, and, some hours later, the flank again being turned, a further retreat took place to the village of Fosse which, with the bridge heads, was held all night and all day of the 10th until 8 p.m., when, after very severe fighting, our meagre forces retired across the River Lawe, blowing up the bridges behind them.

About 1 a.m. of the 11th, the enemy was reported advancing in large numbers down the Lestrem-Zelobes road, showing that he had crossed the Lawe further north, and " B " Coy.'s Lewis gun on our left flank was overwhelmed, the men fighting to the last.

During the day, retiral after retiral took place after stubborn fighting, in each case our left flank being turned, while the enemy machine-gun fire and shelling were very severe. On the morning of the 12th, the enemy was again behind our line in the Bois de Pacaut, but a new line was held until 8 p.m., when, as reinforcements had arrived, the battalions of the 152nd Brigade were withdrawn for reorganization, the 5th Seaforths moving to Witternesse, where it had time to count its losses, which were heavy.

Officers, 3 killed, 6 wounded, 1 missing; other ranks, 17 killed, 109 wounded, 94 missing (majority killed). The officers killed were Lieut. T. Grant, M.C., Lieut. Squires and Lieut. Cameron.

For his magnificent work during this battle Capt. G. A. Sutherland was recommended for the D.S.O., but was awarded the M.C. On arrival with "A" Coy. at Les Huit Maisons, he found King Edward's Horse sorely pressed, the enemy attacking in large numbers covered by heavy fire.

He personally reconnoitred the position, and placed his men so ably that the position was held, and the enemy attacks repulsed. Throughout he displayed magnificent coolness and utter disregard of personal safety.

The battalion scouts and runners did invaluable work in this rather mixed battle. Time and again they went out on reconnaissance work, bringing back most accurate and concise information of our own and the enemy's dispositions. For this work Corpl. Geo. Hotchkiss and Pte. Wm. Anderson were awarded the D.C.M., an honour which was also conferred on L/Corpl. J. Shand for personally bringing a Lewis gun into action on the left of King Edward's Horse, thus repulsing the enemy. He thereafter carried a wounded man to the rear, bringing back a supply of magazines for his gun.

The men of our Division were very galled at the adulatory terms in which the London Press referred to the gallant stand made by the Portuguese, the fact being that the right Portuguese Division made no stand worth mentioning, but fled like hares without rifle or equipment, even without boots. One German prisoner said that, after taking the first trench, they advanced for an hour without the slightest opposition, so great had been the debacle, and for this we had to pay with gallant British lives.

Some of the men belonging to the 152nd Brigade, who were captured during the battle, have a pitiful story to tell as to their treatment by the chivalrous ! Hun, who was always so ready to protest against the supposed unjust treatment of his own men.

These N.C.O.'s and men have assured me that they were not sent to Germany, but were close up to the battlefront until the Armistice was signed. By a curious coincidence some of my own men, as prisoners, were billeted in the house in Laventie in which they had lived in 1915. By this time, Laventie was in the hands of the Huns, but close up to the battlefront, and here they were employed at roadmaking under British shell-fire and aeroplane bombing. The British bombing planes put the fear of death into the Hun, and their armed guard used to run for shelter, while the workparty stood out in the open and cheered lustily, as bomb after bomb dropped in close proximity to them, they seemingly having the feeling that no British bomb could hurt them. This they did until an unlucky bomb one day smashed the leg of one of the party, and thereafter they wisely took cover. Their letters were delivered to them bearing a German prison camp address, but of parcels they saw nothing, although many had been sent.

They were worked 12 to 14 hours per day on a handful of biscuits, a bowl of so-called soup, and a cup or two of *Ersatz* coffee. The result was they became reduced to skeletons, and soon were bootless and in rags. Every weed that could possibly be turned into food was collected from the fields and marshes, which also supplied them with a plentiful supply of frogs. Some men had a number of short strings dangling from their belt hooks, and whenever a frog was espied it was fastened to a string, so that by nightfall they had a bunch of them ready to be converted into a soup or stew. Another young soldier who was severely wounded in one of these battles says that, as he lay on the field, Germans, armed with rifle and bayonet, came out, and every man who seemed too badly wounded to be fit for work for some time was bayoneted where he lay.

This soldier bears eight bayonet stabs about the neck, arms and shoulders, but none chanced to touch a vital spot, and, as he feigned death, the brutal Hun went on to the next man, but, turning back, he kicked him in the face, laying open his cheek bone, and leaving a mark which he will carry as long as he lives.

Next day he was found still alive, and brought to a German hospital, where the doctor, on being told how he had got the eight bayonet wounds, warned him, if he valued his life, to keep silence, or he would never leave Germany alive.

Until 5th May the battalion remained in rest at Witternesse when it relieved the 44th Canadian infantry battalion in the Oppy sector near Neuville-St. Vaast.

Until 11th July the Division held the front between this village and Roclincourt, and the battalion's alternation of duties brought it once again in contact with such well-known spots as Ecurie, Roclincourt, La Maison Blanche and Bailleul, so familiar in the Vimy Ridge offensive in 1917. No general attack was attempted by the enemy in this sector, although artillery and trench-mortar fire were often heavy, and raiding parties sometimes made an attempt upon our lines without success.

The total casualties for two comparatively restful months were: 1 officer wounded, 2 other ranks killed, and 52 wounded or gassed.

On 26th June the battalion was inspected at Roclincourt by General Sir H. S. Horne, K.C.B., K.C.M.G., who presented medals to a number of the men.

On 5th July Lieut.-Col. J. M. Scott, D.S.O., relinquished the command on proceeding to England for six months' rest, his place being taken by Col. W. Morrison, M.C., D.C.M., Gordon Highlanders. Colonel Scott had held command during the very strenuous fighting of the preceding eighteen months, and in his farewell message he expressed his sincere appreciation of the splendid manner in which all ranks had invariably done their duty. He wished them all good luck and was certain that the 5th Seaforths would yet further enhance their high reputation by carrying through all that was entrusted to them.

SECOND BATTLE OF THE MARNE, JULY 1918

In July the French were being hard pressed in the Rheims-Soissons area, and appealed to the British for help, with the result that, among other Divisions, the 51st was withdrawn from the line on 11th July and at once proceeded to entrain for the Epernay area.

After a long, wearisome train journey of over 27 hours, the battalion detrained at Romilly on 15th July and on the 19th they arrived at Champillon (Chalons), and spent the night in the Bois de St. Quentin.

Here our troops found a country vastly different from those other areas of France in which they had fought.

They found a thickly-wooded country of hills and valleys, admirably suited for the machine gun and sniping tactics of the enemy, who had already burst through the French defences, and had firmly established himself in the densely-wooded country behind the French line. The Division was at once moved up to attack in conjunction with the French.

At 8 a.m. on the 21st the 152nd Brigade took part in the attack, the 6th Gordons, with the 5th Seaforths in support, advancing into the Bois de Coutron, which was strongly held by the enemy.

Both battalions met with very stiff opposition, particularly from machine guns and trench mortars, with the result that, after advancing 400 yards, the attack was held up, and the line consolidated there. During the night this position was very heavily shelled, but was held until the following night, when the Brigade was relieved and moved further east to more open ground near Bullin Farm, with its right flank on the River Ardre, a tributary of the Vesle. Here at 6 a.m. on the 23rd the Brigade again attacked, the 5th Sea-

forths on the right next the Ardre, with the 6th Seaforths on their left and a battalion of the 62nd Division
on their right across the river. When " B " and " D "
Companies moved forward, they were met with heavy
enfilade machine-gun fire, but this was speedily over-
come, six machine guns being captured and their
crews either killed or made prisoners.

In connection with this work, Sergt. Sydney Wood
was awarded a D.C.M. for, when his Company was enfiladed by a machine gun, he engaged the crew, killing
one and wounding a second, whereupon he rushed the
gun, capturing the remaining three men.

Another D.C.M. was won by Pte. James Kennedy
who, when his section commander was killed by a
sniper, took command of the section, and, going forward alone, rushed the post, killed the sniper, and
took the section forward, displaying great coolness
and courage under terrific shell-fire during the remainder of the operations.

This advance continued successfully through a small
wood, the Bois de l'Aulney, and the final objective
was gained at 8.20 a.m. with comparatively few casualties, but at 10.30 a.m. a very heavy barrage, continuing
for three hours, was put upon our positions, causing
heavy losses.

In the afternoon the surplus personnel from Champillon were brought up, and on the 24th 100 of the
most exhausted men were sent back to Nanteuil to

rest. On the morning of the 27th, a further advance was begun, the Brigade attack being made by the battalion, now reduced to 8 officers and 250 other ranks.

During this advance, all the officers of the leading Company became casualties, but, perceiving this, Lieut. W. W. Nicolson, in command of the support Company, at once went forward, took command, and led them on to their objective.

By his promptness at a most critical moment he enabled the advance to continue in accordance with time-table. For his courage, coolness, and initiative through the battle, he was decorated with the M.C. and the Croix de Guerre with Palms.

During the 28th the advance still continued, the enemy being pressed back beyond Chaumuzy through the Bois des Eclisses where the attack had been held up on the 21st.

On the night of the 28th the battalion was relieved, and moved back to the vicinity of Bullin Farm where it remained until the 31st collecting and burying its dead from the battlefield. Its losses in eight days of the heaviest fighting it had ever participated in were as follows : officers, 7 killed, 8 wounded ; other ranks, 67 killed, 275 wounded, 12 missing.

Among the officers killed was Capt. W. A. Macdonald who came out with the battalion, and had been badly wounded at Festubert in 1915 and again in 1917.

His bosom friend, Capt. G. A. Sutherland, M.C., was killed a day or two later, so that in death they were not divided. Two typical Highlanders they were, of deep religious principles, cool, calm, and collected in every danger, thinking only of their men and their duty, hating war with a fervent hatred, but determined to do their utmost for right and justice.

The other officers whom the battalion had to mourn were Capt. J. A. St. L. Tredenwick, Lieut. Daniel M. Clyne, and Second Lieuts. A. C. Grossart, A. S. B. Taylor, and D. Shaw, while among N.C.O.'s the old-timers deeply regretted the loss of Coy.-Sergt.-Major James Bruce, D.C.M., " Big Jim Bruce " as he was familiarly known, whose stalwart figure had been so long associated with the battalion that he was regarded as typical of its non-commissioned ranks.

Prior to the Division leaving the 5th French Army, a message was read from General Berthelot, expressing to all ranks the thanks and admiration which their great deeds deserved.

He pointed out that, by constant efforts for ten successive days, the British troops had made themself masters of the Ardre valley which they had freely watered with their blood. They had captured 21 officers and 1300 other ranks, 40 guns, and 140 machine guns, while four enemy Divisions had been broken and repulsed.

Marfaux, Chaumuzy, and Montagne de Bligny,

three famous names, would be written in letters of gold in the annals of the regiments.

On 2nd August, the Division again entrained for the north, the 5th Seaforths arriving at Pernes on the 4th, and embussing for Gauchin Legal where they remained until the 17th.

The Offensive on the Scarpe, August and September 1918

On 18th August the battalion relieved the 2/7 King's Liverpool Regiment in the Fampoux sector, so that once again it was back on the scene of its gallant fights of April and May 1917 associated with the Chemical Works and Roeux. Here we found that, in the interval, our 1917 work had been largely undone, for the enemy had recaptured these two strongholds, and were also in possession of the greater part of Fampoux. The 51st, annoyed that its sacrifices had thus been in vain, volunteered for the difficult task of recapturing this area, an offer which was at once accepted, and with the Canadians on the south side of the Scarpe, they took up the task with right good will. Scarcely was the battalion in the line, when the enemy attempted a raid on a post of the left front company. Private W. Crozier was the sentry over this post when the party attacked, and was shot through the hip by the German officer, but, although badly wounded, he killed the officer and wounded two of his men, before he fell back from his post. Only two men of the post remained unwounded and Pte. Crozier brought up assistance, and thus prevented any of them from being made prisoners, the raid being for identification purposes. For his gallantry he was awarded the D.C.M. On the morning of the 20th, a strong raiding party under Lieut. Dures went out to attack and, if possible, capture a strongly-held sunken road on the north-eastern outskirts of Fampoux. Although repulsed at first, Lieut. Dures reorganized his party, and succeeded in capturing the position. Although heavily shelled all day and fiercely attacked in the evening, they retained their hold, with heavy losses to the enemy. For this excellent piece of work, Lieut. Dures was awarded the M.C., and congratulatory telegrams were received by the battalion from the Brigade, the Divisional and the Corps Commanders.

On the 21st, the battalion again advanced and captured another system of trenches. During this period, our lines were heavily bombarded, principally with gas shells, and gas casualties were severe, but the advance continued steadily, and in six days' fighting the Chemical Works, Roeux, Plouvain, and Greenland Hill, a slightly rising piece of ground north-east of the Chemical Works, were once again in British hands.

THE 1918 CAMPAIGN

Lieut.-General Sir A. W. Currie, K.C.B., K.C.M.G., commanding the Canadian Corps, under whom the 51st Division fought in this battle, in his farewell message to the Division when it left his corps, referred to its old associations with the Canadians at Festubert and Givenchy in 1915 and at Arras in 1917, and concludes as follows : " That your Division was able, after the strenuous fighting in which it has been engaged this year, to take and keep the strong position of Greenland Hill testifies in the strongest possible manner to the fact that the fighting qualities of the 51st are second to none in all the allied armies."

Up to 12th September the battalion continued in the Fampoux sector, holding and strengthening the line, now well in front of Plouvain, there being continued patrol encounters in keeping in touch with the enemy, and in one of these 2nd Lieut. A. G. Montgomery was killed.

The other casualties during this period of strenuous fighting were comparatively slight, 10 other ranks being killed and 33 wounded, while 4 officers and 117 other ranks were gassed.

On 12th September the Division was relieved by the 49th, and the battalion went back to Petit Servins where it remained until the 23rd, returning to the same sector, but on 2nd October the Division finally left the valley of the Scarpe, the battalion going into camp at Acq.

WAR DIARY OF THE FIFTH SEAFORTHS

FINAL BRITISH OFFENSIVE, OCTOBER–NOVEMBER 1918

On 6th October a move was made by motor-lorry to the Queant area, and on the 10th the 43rd Canadian Highlanders were relieved in Bourlon Wood near Cambrai. By this date the Canadians, with great gallantry and determination, had captured Cambrai, and driven the enemy beyond it, and were now being relieved, the 51st Division taking over part of their front.

On the 12th the British advance was renewed, the 152nd Brigade participating, the objective being a line east of Avesnes-le-Sec. The 5th Seaforths were on the right with the 6/7th Gordons on their left, the 6th Seaforths being in support.

At midday the barrage opened and ten minutes later the infantry advanced and in two hours gained all their objectives.

The advance was resumed at 9 a.m. of the 13th, the objective being the eastern edges of Le Grand Bois and Bois de Lentre and thence to eastern outskirts of Noyelles.

Immediately prior to our advance, the enemy put a heavy artillery and machine-gun barrage down on our line, but in spite of that and heavy enemy resistance, and also in spite of the fact that there was no British barrage, the battalion advanced a considerable distance until held up by enfilade fire, from which it suffered heavily. As the battalions on the right and left found it impossible to come up and get in touch, at 2 p.m. a slight retiral took place, and here again the casualties were severe. During this retiral, 2nd Lieut. T. S. Hennessy with about 20 men remained out in front, and successfully withstood all enemy counter-attacks. He thus gave time for the remainder of the battalion to withdraw, and to be reorganized in its new position. He held stubbornly on until dusk when he safely withdrew his men. For this gallant work he was awarded the M.C. Many brave deeds were done in this open warfare.

L/Sergt. Hector MacKenzie, who had won the D.C.M. in Mesopotamia, was awarded a bar for gallant and invaluable service on the 13th.

When the left of the line began to waver under heavy machine-gun fire, he ran across from the right of the line, a distance of over 200 yards, under very heavy fire, rallied and encouraged the men and formed a defensive flank.

Stretcher-bearer James MacKenzie, on the same date, went out on five separate occasions and brought in wounded under very heavy fire, working continuously for ten hours, although he himself was wounded and gassed. On another occasion he heard a wounded man's cries, and had just got to him when a shell burst near and buried him. In spite of his own injuries, he

M

lifted the wounded man, and carried him in until he died in his arms.

Coy.-Sergt.-Major Wm. Macbeath steadied his company when severely shaken by heavy machine-gun fire, and continued to do so after being badly wounded, setting a fine example by his utter disregard of his own personal safety.

Sergt. John Dunbar inspired and steadied his men under terrific fire, and later in the day went out to bring in a wounded man, but was badly wounded when half-way out.

L/Corpl. Donald Omand, owing to heavy officer and N.C.O. casualties was left in charge of a platoon, and set such a splendid example, by moving freely among them under heavy fire, that he kept them advancing, and got them to establish posts, and even after being wounded he refused to go to the Aid Post, remaining on duty till badly gassed the following day.

Such deeds as these are but a few, a very few, of many, but they are sufficient to show the spirit which animated all ranks in this, the concluding struggle against the Hun, who, in spite of all that has been said to the contrary, was fighting as he had never fought before, in trying to stem the successful allied advance, which, however, would not be gainsaid.

The line remained fast during the 14th, 15th and 16th, and on the 17th the battalion was relieved, and went into reserve at Thun-St. Martin.

THE 1918 CAMPAIGN

On the 24th it was once more in the line which in the interval had been considerably advanced, the new position being on the Thiant-Monchaux road.

Here at 7 a.m. of the 25th the 152nd and 153rd Brigades were launched to the attack with the 4th Division on their right. On this occasion the 5th Seaforths were in support, and, in spite of a heavy enemy barrage, all objectives were gained by midday.

At 10 a.m. of the 26th the advance was continued, and again all objectives were gained by noon.

At 4 p.m. the enemy launched a heavy counter-attack which was successfully held up, and the line was consolidated, the battalion being finally relieved on the 28th when it went back to Thun-St. Martin.

During these 16 days' fighting the casualties were : 2 officers, 2nd Lieuts. R. Tolmie and W. Leggat, killed, and 12 wounded, while of other ranks 66 were killed, 333 wounded and 9 missing.

This battle marks the finish of the 5th Seaforths' fighting record, for from the 28th October till the Armistice was signed on 11th November the battalion lay in rest at Thun-St. Martin. Armistice Day was observed as a battalion holiday, there being a Company cross-country run in the afternoon, a concert by the " Balmorals," the Divisional concert party, in the evening, and thereafter a fireworks display and bonfire.

WAR DIARY OF THE FIFTH SEAFORTHS

On 19th November Prince Albert visited and inspected the battalion.

Educational classes were formed and, until the battalion was broken up, were carried on very successfully.

In December Col. W. Morrison returned from England and resumed command from Col. J. Reid, M.C., of the 7th Royal Highlanders who had held the command since 14th October.

In January a move was made to Houdeng Aimeries in Belgium, and here the command was taken by Col. A. L. Macmillan, T.D., who had come out with the battalion as junior Major in 1915, and had for some time been in command of a battalion of the Royal Scottish Fusiliers. From January onwards the battalion strength was gradually reduced owing to drafts being sent to the Army of Occupation on the Rhine and to parties being sent to Dispersal Camps for demobilization, until by 8th March it was at Cadre strength.

On 10th April the Cadre embarked at Dunkirk for Southampton whence they entrained to Gailes on the 13th, and on the 15th they arrived at Golspie, the headquarters of the battalion, where they received a right royal welcome from the inhabitants.

THE END